Primarily Bears
Grades K-6
A Collection of Elementary Activities

EDITORS

Arthur Wiebe
AIMS Program Director
Fresno Pacific College

Dave Youngs
Assistant Program Director
Fresno Pacific College

Judith Hillen
AIMS Program Director
Fresno Pacific College

Kim Sutton
Assistant Program Director
AIMS Education Foundation

WRITING TEAM

Aviva Berdugo
Elementary Teacher
Temple Emanuel Day School
Beverly Hills, California

Daneen Glasser
Elementary Teacher
Fountain Valley Elementary School District

Maureen Allen
Science Resource Specialist
Irvine Unified School District

Pat McConnell
Secondary Math and Science Teacher
Whittier School District

Susan Jones
Elementary Teacher
Fountain Valley Elementary School District

Illustrator and Contributing Editor
Sheryl Mercier
Fresno Unified School District

AIMS (**A**ctivities **I**ntegrating **M**athematics and **S**cience) began in 1981 with a grant from the National Science Foundation. The non-profit AIMS Education Foundation publishes hands-on instructional materials (books and the monthly AIMS Newsletter) that integrate curricular disciplines such as mathematics, science, language arts, and social studies. The Foundation sponsors a national program of professional development through which educators may gain both an understanding of the AIMS philosophy and expertise in teaching by integrated, hands-on methods.

TABLE OF CONTENTS

INTRODUCTION

Primarily Bears invites the child within us to experience a variety of advanced mathematics concepts in a simple, gentle manner, via the lovable Teddy Bear. The activities range from simple to sophisticated and may be appropriate for a wide range of grade levels. Highly motivating concepts include logic, permutations and arrangements, probability and statistics, and measurement and graphing.

This collection of elementary activities begins with a series of over twenty logic problems that place logical thinking and problem solving in the real world. Using plastic Teddy Bear Counters in four different colors, students have a tool with which to make a non-permanent record of responses in a matrix to find solutions to situational math and science problems similar to those encountered by the scientist. The logic explored introduces students to the many aspects of symmetry, patterns, and sequence and the mathematical power that accompanies the recognition of patterns in problem solving.

Following the logic sequence students will delight in dressing Teddy Bears for the seasons by exploring the various combinations and arrangements of attire for Terri and Teddy in **Teddy Bears Dress for Summer, Fall, Winter, and Spring.** Some students will be able to discover and understand the generalization while others will simply picture a new arrangement and search for another.

Young students will enjoy a first look at probability and statistics and make predictions about a random sample of bears in **Teddy Bears Playing in the Den.**

Beginning measurement and graphing experiences are captured in **Teddy Bear Clubs Go Weighing, Let Me Count the Ways, and Teddy Bears and Oranges.** Often overlooked, estimation, receives its just rewards in **The Jar That Likes to Keep You Guessing.** Students and teachers alike enjoy this activity throughout the year. . .over and over again. Gummy Bears, M&Ms® Candies, and Jelly Beans may have their beginning in the "guessing jar" and then move very conveniently into the wonderful world of graphing.

It is the desire of the writers of these activities that both the teacher and the learner enjoy math and science and share the wonder of experiencing science first hand.

I HEAR, AND I FORGET
I SEE, AND I REMEMBER
I DO, AND I UNDERSTAND

-Chinese Proverb

Index of Skills

MATH SKILLS

SCIENCE PROCESSES

Teddy Bears Go to the Movies and Teddy Bears Go Hiking

I. Topic Area
Sequencing and patterning.

II. Introductory Statement
Students will use Teddy Bear counters or other objects to form and repeat a pattern.

III. Math Skills

a. Discovering or designing a pattern
b. Sequencing

Science Processes

a. Observing
b. Drawing conclusions
c. Applying

IV. Key Question
Can you find the pattern and repeat it to the end of the line?

V. Background Information
Since both mathematics and science involve studies in patterns it is important to provide an abundance of practice in their discovery and replication. In these lessons students will study patterns at an elementary level.

Each of the activity pages may be used for a variety of patterns.

The line-up in each instance is curved rather than in a straight line. This forces students to pay strict attention to the original pattern as repetitions are formed.

The first decision to make is that of determining who will create the pattern: the teacher, the student working alone, or a student in a cooperative learning group. Each of these has a specific value.

The second decision involves the length of the pattern. "Teddy Bears Go to the Movies" has 12 spaces. Any divisor of 12 is suitable for the length of the pattern since this will result in the completion of the final repetition of the pattern in the final space. Therefore, patterns of 2, 3, 4, or 6 objects are appropriate. Since in "Teddy Bears Go Hiking" there are 15 spaces, the length of the pattern should be either 3 or 5.

The third step is to choose the types of objects to be used. Although designed with Teddy Bear counters in mind, other objects such as buttons may be substituted.

Finally, the shape of a single instance of the pattern must be determined. Many possibilities suggest themselves. If we think in terms of colored Teddy Bear counters then color alone becomes the basis of the pattern. With a three-object sequence using red and blue, for example, choices such as red-red-blue, red-blue-red, blue-red-red, blue-red-blue, red-blue-blue, and blue-blue-red are possible.

As students become more adept, the length of the sequence may be increased.

VI. Management Suggestions
These activities may be done as free exploration where students create a pattern and then replicate it as often as possible. Using this approach, students will discover that patterns of a certain length will "come out even" and others not, an experience in finding factors of twelve or fifteen.

On the other hand, the teacher or a student may instruct everyone in a group or the entire class how to construct the initial pattern.

VII. Procedure
1. Determine how the class will be organized for this activity.
2. Select the objects to be used.
3. Determine who will select the initial pattern.
4. Have students compare and discuss their solutions

VIII. Discussion Questions
1. What length patterns resulted in the line-up coming out even when using "Teddy Bears Go to the Movies"?
2. What length patterns came out even using "Teddy Bears Go Hiking"? What kind of numbers are these? (divisors or factors)

.

COST: 1 POT HONEY

NOW PLAYING
Teddy Bears
in
Space

The Teddy Bears
Go to the Movies

HONEY

HONEY

PRIMARILY BEARS, BOOK 1

2

© 1987 AIMS Education Foundation

The Teddy Bears Go Hiking

Who's Not Home?

I. Topic Area
Patterning and logical reasoning

II. Introductory Statement
In the following activities students will determine what color Teddy Bears belong in each of the blank spaces of the matrix by noting the pattern of the bears that are at home.

III. Math Skills
a. Discovering a pattern
b. Observing symmetry
c. Extending a matrix pattern
d. Using logic

Science Processes
a. Observing
b. Interpreting data
c. Inferring
d. Applying

IV. Materials
A supply of Teddy Bears or pictures of Teddy Bears in the indicated colors
Student worksheet

V. Key Question
What color Teddy Bear lives in each of the empty homes?

VI. Background Information
This series of activities follows a common theme: discovering the color pattern represented by the Teddy Bears who are at home, generalizing that pattern, and using it to determine the color of the Teddy Bears who are not at home.

Often, these are studies in symmetry. Several types of symmetry should be noted. First, line symmetry is that in which the pattern could be simulated by a mirror. That is, if the mirror is placed somewhere in the pattern it shows in the reflection what color Teddy Bear(s) should be placed in a certain position. For example, suppose we have the following pattern:

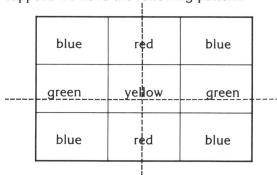

blue	red	blue
green	yellow	green
blue	red	blue

If we place a mirror vertically through the center as shown by the vertical line and look into the mirror from the left side, we see a pattern in the mirror that is the same as what is behind the mirror to the right.

Similarly, if we place the mirror on the horizontal line through the center of the pattern and look at it from the bottom, we see in the mirror the pattern that lies behind the mirror above the line.

Whenever we can place a mirror through the center of a pattern in some manner and see in the mirror what is behind the mirror we have line symmetry.

The above pattern also has point or rotational symmetry. The point in this case is in the center of the square occupied by a yellow Teddy Bear. Note that if you proceed from any color through the center square to the third square, its occupant will be on the same color as that in the first square. The rotational symmetry is demonstrated by the fact that the pattern in this case can be rotated 90 degrees each time and the same color pattern as existed originally reappears.

Students may find other patterns which can be logically explained that are not necessarily symmetrical, for example, a checkerboard arrangement. This is acceptable as long as a logical explanation can be given, but the pattern that is explained must be applicable throughout the arrangement.

Matrices are used often in science for classification as well as in mathematics. These activities fit well into that part of the science curriculum which deals with classification through the use of matrices.

VII. Management Suggestions
1. Divide the students into groups of two or more. This is to encourage discussion among the students about the color of the missing Teddy Bears. They need to agree that the pattern they have selected is consistent throughout the arrangement.
2. Provide each group with a sufficient number of Teddy Bears of each color and the student worksheet.
3. Have students defend their pattern by describing the pattern and using logic to explain their solution.
4. Accept any solution which is supported by sound logic.

VIII. What the Students Will Do
1. Discover the pattern.
2. Fill the missing homes with Teddy Bears of the correct color.
3. Describe the pattern they discovered and defend it by recording their explanation.

Who's Not Home Continued...

X. Discussion

Have students share their solutions and discuss the reasons behind them. One of the major objectives of these activities is to use logical reasoning.

In general, one way that the patterns can be determined is by observing either line or point symmetry. A line of symmetry acts like a mirror, reflecting behind it what occurs before it. In point symmetry, moves of the same distance but in opposite directions from a central point result in landing on objects of the same kind.

Cave 1: This has both point and line symmetry. There is a yellow line (row) through the center both horizontally and vertically. Therefore, colors would reflect about both such lines. The point symmetry consists of the center space being yellow. Movement in opposite directions, for example diagonally, for the same distance will land the object on bears with like colors.

Cave 2 has point symmetry with respect to the blue bear in the center.

Cave 3 has point symmetry with respect to the yellow bear in the center and line symmetry with respect to the yellow diagonal array on the one hand or the red-yellow-red diagonal on the other.

Cave 4 has point symmetry with respect to the blue bear in the center and line symmetry with respect to the center vertical arrangement of blue-blue-blue.

Cave 5 has point symmetry with respect to the center red bear and line symmetry with respect to the green-red-green diagonal and the blue-red-blue diagonal.

Cave 6 has point symmetry with respect to the center yellow and two line symmetries: about the center green-yellow-green vertical line and the horizontal red-yellow-red line.

Cave 7 is symmetric with respect to the center red and the two diagonal lines, both of which are yellow-red-yellow. It is also symmetric with respect to the two center lines, vertically and horizontally: both blue-red-blue.

Cave 8 has point symmetry about the center green and line symmetry about the two diagonals.

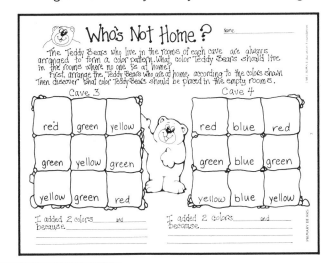

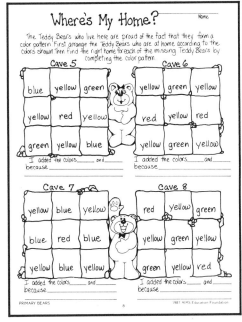

© 1987 AIMS Education Foundation

Who's Not Home?

Name: _____

The Teddy Bears who live in the rooms of each cave are always arranged to form a color pattern. What color Teddy Bears should live in the rooms where no one is at home? First, arrange the Teddy Bears who are at home, according to the colors shown. Then discover what color Teddy Bears should be placed in the empty rooms.

Cave 1

red	yellow	yellow
yellow	yellow	yellow
red	yellow	red

I added 2 colors _____ and _____ because _____

Cave 2

blue	red	blue
red	blue	blue
red	blue	

I added 2 colors _____ and _____ because _____

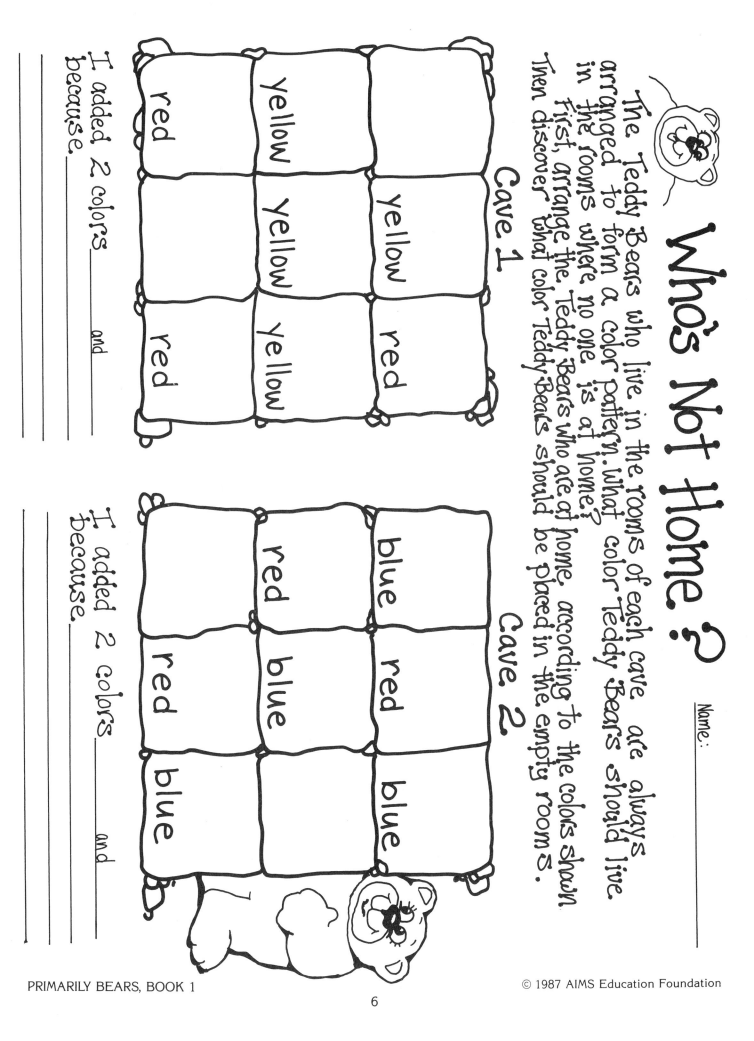

PRIMARILY BEARS, BOOK 1

© 1987 AIMS Education Foundation

6

Who's Not Home?

Name: _____

The Teddy Bears who live in the rooms of each cave are always arranged to form a color pattern. What color Teddy Bears should live in the rooms where no one is at home?

First, arrange the Teddy Bears who are at home, according to the colors shown. Then discover what color Teddy Bears should be placed in the empty rooms.

Cave 3

red	green	yellow
green	yellow	
yellow	green	

I added 2 colors _____ and _____
because _____

Cave 4

red	blue	
green	blue	green
blue		yellow

I added 2 colors _____ and _____
because _____

Where's My Home?

The Teddy Bears who live here are proud of the fact that they form a color pattern. First arrange the Teddy Bears who are at home according to the colors shown. Then find the right home for each of the missing Teddy Bears by completing the color pattern.

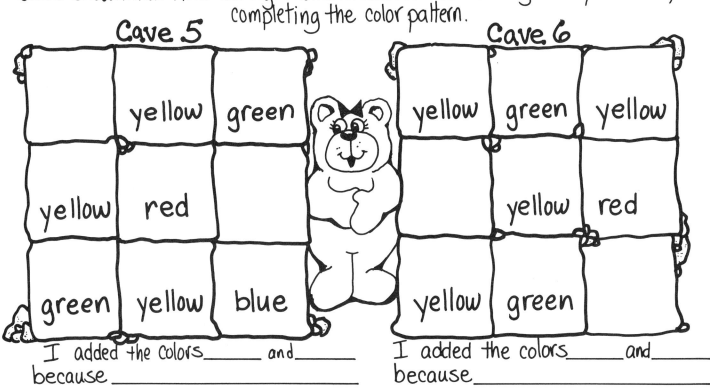

Cave 5

	yellow	green
yellow	red	
green	yellow	blue

I added the colors _____ and _____
because _____
_____

Cave 6

yellow	green	yellow
	yellow	red
yellow	green	

I added the colors _____ and _____
because _____
_____

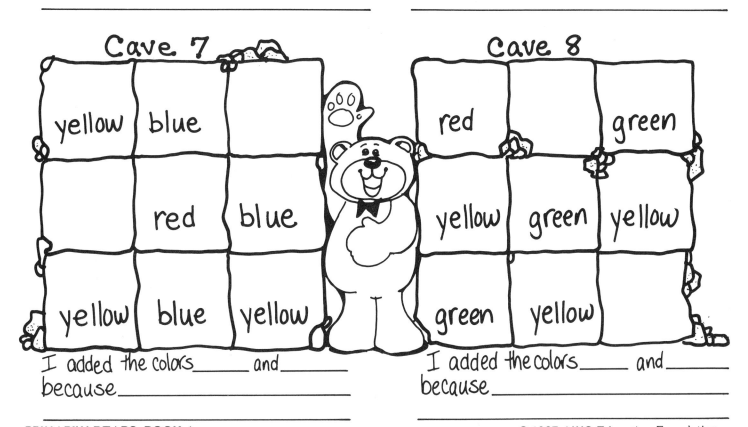

Cave 7

yellow	blue	
	red	blue
yellow	blue	yellow

I added the colors _____ and _____
because _____
_____

Cave 8

red		green
yellow	green	yellow
green	yellow	

I added the colors _____ and _____
because _____
_____

Teddy Bears in a Parade, etc.

This sequence of activities is an extension of the preceding ones and the general procedure is the same. However, the patterns become progressively more challenging.

The solutions for each are given below. Students should be encouraged to discuss how they found their solutions. Any solution, even if different from those shown here, which is consistent throughout the arrangement is acceptable. There will be few if any exceptions, however, to the patterns shown.

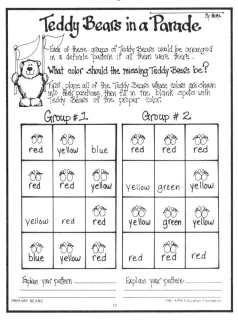

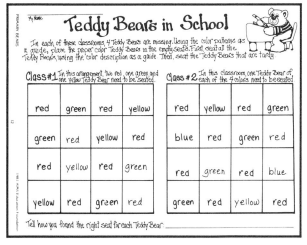

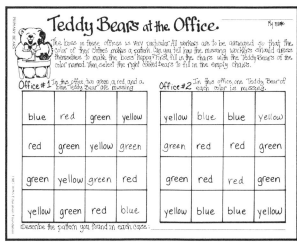

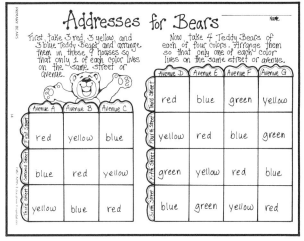

© 1987 AIMS Education Foundation

Teddy Bears in a Parade

My Name

Each of these groups of Teddy Bears would be arranged in a definite pattern if all them were there.

What color should the missing Teddy Bears be?

First, place all of the Teddy Bears whose colors are shown into their positions, then fill in the blank spots with Teddy Bears of the proper color.

Group #1

red	yellow	
red	red	yellow
		red
blue	yellow	red

Group #2

red	red	red
		yellow
yellow	green	yellow
	red	

Explain your pattern: _____

_____

Teddy Bear Marching Bands

These Teddy Bears are special. They arrange themselves into a definite pattern of colors.

What color should the missing Teddy Bears be?

First, place all of the Teddy Bears whose colors are shown into position. Then fill in the blank spots with the color of Teddy Bears needed to complete the pattern.

BAND # 1

blue	yellow	green
red	blue	
	red	blue
	green	red

BAND # 2

red	green	
yellow	blue	yellow
	blue	yellow
red		red

Explain your pattern: _____

_____

Explain your pattern: _____

_____

My Name _____

Teddy Bears in School

In each of these classrooms, 4 Teddy Bears are missing. Using the color patterns as a guide, place the proper color Teddy Bears in the empty seats. First, seat all the Teddy Bears, using the color description as a guide. Then, seat the Teddy Bears that are tardy.

Class #1 In this arrangement, two red one green and one yellow Teddy Bear need to be seated.

red	green	red	yellow
green		yellow	red
red	yellow	red	green
yellow	red	green	

Class #2 In this classroom, one Teddy Bear of each of the 4 colors need to be seated.

red	yellow	red	green
blue	red	green	
red		red	red
green	red		red

Tell how you found the right seat for each Teddy Bear: _____

Teddy Bears at the Office.

My name _____

The boss in these offices is very particular. All workers are to be arranged so that the color of their clothes makes a pattern. Can you tell how the missing workers should dress themselves to make the boss happy? First, fill in the chairs with the Teddy Bears of the color named. Then, select the right colored bears to fill in the empty chairs.

Office #1 In this office, two green, a red, and a blue Teddy Bear are missing.

blue	green	yellow	
red	green	yellow	red
green	yellow		
yellow	green	red	

Office #2 In this office, one Teddy Bear of each color is missing.

yellow	blue		
	red	red	green
green	red		green
yellow	blue	blue	yellow

Describe the pattern you found in each case: _____

Addresses for Bears

First, take 3 red, 3 yellow, and 3 blue Teddy Bears and arrange them in these 9 houses so that only 1 of each color lives on the same street or avenue.

Now, take 4 Teddy Bears of each of four colors. Arrange them so that only one of each color lives on the same street or avenue.

Name _____

	Third Street	Second Street	First Street
Avenue A			
Avenue B			
Avenue C			

	Sixth Street	Fifth Street	Fourth Street	Third Street
Avenue D				
Avenue E				
Avenue F				
Avenue G				

PRIMARILY BEARS, BOOK 1

Bear Caves and Bear Baseball

I. **Topic Area**
   Logic and problem solving.

II. **Introductory Statement**
   Students will use Teddy Bear counters and logical thinking skills to solve situational problems.

III. **Math Skills**   **Science Processes**
   a. Logical thinking   a. Comparing
   b. Sequencing   b. Organizing & recording data
   c. Problem solving   c. Inductive & deductive reasoning
   d. Inferring   d. Drawing conclusions

IV. **Materials**
   Teddy Bear counters or pictures of Teddy Bear counters
   Crayons or colored pencils

V. **Key Question**
   Which bear lives in which cave? (Key question will vary with each logic problem.)

VI. **Background Information**
   Youngsters in the early grades should have many opportunities to make reasonable or logical conjectures about situations with concrete materials. Every child should be involved in hands-on activities that allow him to verbalize and describe or act out the situation described (the problem. Through discussion and careful questioning on the part of the teacher, students may see relationships, implications, and make observations, generalizations, predictions, and interpretations.

   Students may use Teddy Bear counters or pictures of Teddy Bears to assist in solving the problems. A bear is placed in each and every square in the grid. Removing bears from the grid is a way of recording a "no" response to a given clue. Bears left in position at the end of the problem indicates a "yes" response. Only one bear should remain in each row and column.

   The questions posed in this manuscript are general in nature and may be appropriate for all of the logic problems in this series. It is important that teachers re-form the questions to be more specific for each activity. For instance, in the Bear Caves problem, what does the clue that states Bonnie does not live in Creaky Cave tell us? What does that clue tell us about Bobby or Burt? These questions are more specific to the problem. In the manuscript the questions are generic, i.e., What does a clue with the word "not" in it tell us?

VII. **Management Suggestions**
   1. This activity may take up to 30-40 minutes.
   2. Students may work in pairs or small groups. First time exposed to simple logic problems may require a highly structured, teacher directed experience.
   3. Overhead projector and a transparency of the problem and grid may be helpful when discussing questions and possible situations.
   4. If Teddy Bear counters are unavailable, use pictures of Teddy Bears and have youngsters cut out one bear for each square on the grid.

VIII. **Procedure**
   1. Distribute activity page and Teddy Bear counters or pictures to each group.
   2. Place one Teddy Bear counter or picture in each space on the grid. All bears in a single row represent the named bear on the left. For instance, in Bear Caves the top row of bears represents Bonnie Bear.
   3. Read the situation together.
   4. Have one student in each group re-tell the situation or problem to his group.
   5. Discuss each clue with the students and the information it provides.
   6. Remove bears as appropriate.
   7. Record conclusions.

IX. **Discussion Questions**
   1. What does a sentence or clue with the word "not" tell you? If "not" tells you that something is not true, how might it also tell you something that is true?
   2. What kinds of words signal a "yes" response?
   3. What kinds of words signal a "no" response?
   4. After discovering a "yes" response, how does that affect the remaining choices in the row? in the column? in the rest of the grid?

X. **Extended Activities**
   Read **Goldilocks and the Three Bears, Paddington Bear** and **Winnie the Pooh.** Write appropriate inquiries as a group experience.

XI. **Solutions**
   Bear Caves, Page 17
   This very elementary activity is a simple introduction to the type of logical reasoning used in this series.

   Since Betty does not live in the Crystal Cave, the Teddy Bear is removed from that cave and opposite Betty. This leaves only the Whispering Cavern as an option for Betty. Since Betty and Barney live next door to each other and not in the same cave, Barney must line in Crystal Cave.

   Students should have abundant opportunities to share their reasoning with other students.

   In this type of exercise, all of the implications of each statement should be discussed and utilized.
   Bear Caves, Page 18
   The key statement may well be the last which introduces the concept of "between." It places Burt in Creaky Cave. Since Bobby does not live in Boulder Bluff (Statement 3) and cannot live in Creaky Cave with Burt (Statement 1) he must live in Honey Comb Cavern. This leaves Boulder Bluff as the residence of Bonnie.

   Bear Baseball, Page 19
   Statement 1 rules out both Buddy and Bobo as the shortstop. By the process of elimination, the shortstop must be Brooke.

   Statement 2 rules out Bobo and Brooke as the pitcher. However, we already know that Brooke is the shortstop. Now Bobo is neither the shortstop (Statement 1) or the pitcher (Statement 2). Therefore, he must be the catcher.

   Buddy is the only remaiining possibility for the position of pitcher. Statement 3 is redundant but was inserted to provide a supplementary clue.

Bear Caves

Clues:

1. Betty Bear and Barney Bear live in caves next door to each other.

2. Betty does not live in Crystal Cave.

3. In which cave do they live?

	Crystal Cave	Whispering Cavern
Betty		
Barney		

Betty lives in _____.

Barney lives in _____.

Bear Caves

Name _____

1. Bonnie, Bobby, and Burt all live in different caves.
2. Bonnie does not live in Creaky Cave.
3. Bobby does not live in Boulder Bluff.
4. Burt lives between Bonnie and Bobby.
   In which caves do they live?

	1. Honey Comb Cavern	2. Creaky Cave	3. Boulder Bluff
Bonnie			
Bobby			
Burt			

Bonnie Bear lives in _____.

Bobby Bear lives in _____.

Burt Bear lives in _____.

Bear Baseball

1. Buddy and the shortstop gave a party for Bobo yesterday.
2. Bobo sent thank you notes to Brooke and the pitcher.
3. Buddy is not the catcher.
4. Who plays each position?

	Catcher	Pitcher	Shortstop
Buddy			
Bobo			
Brooke			

Buddy Bear is the _____.

Bobo Bear is the _____.

Brooke Bear is the _____.

Bear Soccer, etc.

(Bear Soccer, Who's Who?, Bears Come to School, Bear Jobs, Bear Breakfast, Teddy Bears Go on Vacation, Bears Play on Wheels, Bear Royalty)

I. Topic Area
Logic and problem solving.

II. Introductory Statement
Students will use Teddy Bear counters and logical thinking skills to solve situational problems.

III. Math Skills
a. Logical thinking
b. Sequencing
c. Problem solving
d. Inferring

Science Processes
a. Comparing
b. Organizing and recording data
c. Inductive and deductive reasoning
d. Drawing conclusions

IV. Materials
Teddy Bear counters or pictures of Teddy Bear counters, crayons or colored pencils

V. Key Question
Which bear plays each position on the Bear soccer team?

VI. Background Information
Youngsters in the early grades should have many opportunities to make reasonable or logical conjectures about situations with concrete materials. Every child should be involved in hands-on activities that allow him to verbalize and describe or act out the situation described (the problem). Through discussion and careful questioning on the part of the teacher, students may see relationships, and make observations, generalizations, predictions, and interpretations.

Students may use Teddy Bear counters or pictures of Teddy Bears to assist in solving the problems. A bear is placed in each and every square in the grid. Removing bears from the grid are a way of recording a "no" response to a given clue. Bears left in position at the end of the problem indicate a "yes" response. Only one bear should remain in each row and column.

The questions posed in this manuscript are general in nature and may be appropriate for all of the logic problems in this series. It is important that teachers re-form the questions to be more specific for each activity. For instance, in the Bear Soccer problem, what does the clue that states Buddy is not the Fullback tell us? What does that clue tell us about Bobo or Brooke? These questions are more specific to the problem. In the manuscript the questions are generic, i.e., What does a clue with the word "not" in it tell us?

VII. Management Suggestions
1. This activity may take up to 30-40 minutes.
2. Students may work in pairs or small groups. First exposure to simple logic problems may require a highly structured, teacher directed experience.
3. Overhead projector and a transparency of the problem and grid may be helpful when discussing questions and possible situations.
4. If Teddy Bear counters are unavailable, use pictures of Teddy Bears and have youngsters cut out one bear for each square grid.

VIII. Procedure
1. Distribute activity page and Teddy Bear counters or pictures to each group.
2. Place one Teddy Bear counter or picture in each space on the grid.
3. Read the situation together.
4. Have one student in each group re-tell the situation or problem to his group.
5. Discuss each clue with the students and the information it provides.
6. Remove bears as appropriate.
7. Record conclusions.

IX. Discussion Questions
1. What does a sentence or clue with the word "not" tell you? If "not" tells you that something is not true, how might it also tell you something that is true?
2. What kinds of words signal a "yes" response?
3. What kinds of words signal a "no" response?
4. After discovering a "yes" response, how does that affect the remaining choices in the row? in the column? the rest of the grid?

X. Solutions, etc.
Bear Soccer
Students may arrive at the result in one of several ways. This is the first:

Buddy and Brooke could not be the forward since they took the forward out to dinner.

Since Buddy is not the fullback, he must be halfback.

This leaves Brooke as the fullback.

Therefore Bobo must be the forward.

A second possibility is this:

Since neither Buddy or Brooke is the forward who is taken out to dinner, Bobo must be the forward.

Since Buddy is not the fullback, the only remaining choice is halfback.

This leaves Brooke as the fullback.

Who's Who?
1. Betty cannot have the last name of Berry (Statement 1).
2. Betty does not have a last name of Black (Statement 2).
3. Therefore, Betty's last name is Brown.
4. Since Burt is not related to Betty he cannot have a last name of Berry. He must be Burt Black.
5. This leaves Barney with the last name of Berry.

Bears Come to School

1. Brooke must be the bear that walks (Statement 1).
2. Buddy does not ride the bus (and does not walk); therefore, he rides the bike (Statement 2).
3. By elimination, this leaves Bobo as the rider of the bus.

Bear Jobs

1. Bernadette must be the dentist (Statement 3).
2. Brittany is not the librarian and cannot be the dentist (Statement 2). Therefore, Brittany must be the astronaut.
3. This leaves Bingo as the librarian.

Bear Breakfast

1. Bernadette must have eaten berries since that is the only food that grows on bushes.
2. Since Bingo did not have cereal with milk (Statement 2) and did not eat berries, he must have eaten honey.
3. This means that Brittany had oatmeal for breakfast. (It is assumed that the oatmeal was eaten with milk.)

Teddy Bears Go on Vacation

1. Barney must travel by either car or train (Statement 1).
2. Bonnie must travel by car (Statement 3).
3. Therefore, Barney must travel by train.
4. Betty likes speed and therefore chooses the plane. (Statement 2).
5. This leaves Burt to travel by boat.

Bears Play on Wheels

1. Bonnie must play on the bicycle or roller skates (eight wheels). (Statement 1).
2. Since Bonnie (Statement 2) and Burt (Statement 3) have fewer wheels than Betty, Betty must play on roller skates.
3. This leaves only the bicycle as a choice for Bonnie.
4. The skateboard and wagon are left. Since Barney's toy is more dangerous to ride than Burt's, he must ride the skateboard.
5. This leaves the wagon to Burt.

Bear Royalty

1. Katie is not the princess or the king. Since she cannot be a prince, she must be the queen.
2. Keith is not the king or the princess, so must be the prince.
3. Kurt cannot be the princess, so must be the king.
4. Karla must be the princess.

Bear Soccer

Buddy, Bobo, and Brooke play on a soccer team. Their positions are halfback, fullback, and forward. Buddy and the forward took Brooke out to dinner after practice last night. Buddy is not the fullback.

Who plays each position?

	Fullback	Halfback	Forward
Buddy			
Brooke			
Bobo			

Bobo plays the _____.

Brooke plays the _____.

Buddy plays the _____.

PRIMARILY BEARS, BOOK 1

© 1987 AIMS Education Foundation

Who's Who?

The first names of the three Teddy Bears are Betty, Barney, and Burt. The last names, not in the same order are Black, Brown, and Berry.
Use these clues to tell Who's Who.

1. Berry is Betty's uncle.
2. Betty's last name is not Black.
3. Burt is not related to Barney or Betty.

	Betty	Barney.	Burt
Black			
Brown			
Berry			

Write a sentence to explain who is who.

_____

_____

Bears Come to School

Buddy, Bobo, and Brooke come to school in 3 different ways:
by bus, on foot, or by bicycle.

Clues: 1. Brooke lives too far from school to walk and
does not ride a bike.
2. Buddy does not ride a bus.
3. Bobo and his friend ride to school.

	Bus	Walk	Bike
Bobo			
Brooke			
Buddy			

How does each bear get to school?

Name: _____ Name: _____ Name: _____

Bear Jobs

Who has each profession?

1. Bernadette is afraid of heights and does not like to fly.
2. Brittany likes to read but does not work at the library.
3. Bernadette advises everyone to "brush 3 times a day."

	Astronaut	Dentist	Librarian
Bernadette			
Brittany			
Bingo			

Bernadette Bear is the _____.

Brittany Bear is the _____.

Bingo Bear is the _____.

Bear Breakfast

Brittany, Bingo, and Bernadette Bear each ate something different for breakfast.

1. Bernadette Bear did not eat anything made by bees.
2. Bingo did not have cereal with milk.
3. Bernadette's breakfast grew on bushes.

	Honey	Oatmeal	Berries
Brittany			
Bingo			
Bernadette			

Brittany Bear ate _____.

Bingo Bear ate _____.

Bernadette Bear ate _____.

Teddy Bears Go On Vacation

Each of these Teddy Bears has a different favorite mode of travel.

Clues:
1. Barney likes to stay close to the ground when travelling.
2. Bonnie and her family like to go camping as they travel.
3. Betty likes to get places as fast as possible.

How did each bear travel?

	Car	Boat	Plane	Train
Betty				
Barney				
Burt				
Bonnie				

Name: _____   Name: _____   Name: _____   Name: _____

Bears Play on Wheels

Four bears, Betty, Barney, Burt, and Bonnie, like to play on toys with wheels.

Clues:
1. Bonnie's toy does not have 4 wheels.
2. Barney's is more dangerous to ride than Burt's so he wears a helmet.
3. Betty's toy has more wheels than Bonnie's.
4. Burt's has fewer wheels than Betty's.

	skateboard	wagon	bicycle	roller skates
Betty				
Barney				
Burt				
Bonnie				

Match the bears with their favorite toy.

Betty: _____   Barney: _____   Burt: _____   Bonnie: _____

Name: _____

Bear Royalty

Katie, Karla, Keith, and Kurt are a King, a prince, a queen, and a princess in the Crystal Kingdom of Bears. Katie and the princess beat Keith and the King in a royal game of monopoly.

Draw what you think each bear looks like.

What is each bear's rank in the Royal Crystal Kingdom?

	King	Queen	Prince	Princess
Katie				
Karla				
Keith				
Kurt				

Katie is the _____. Keith is the _____.
Karla is the _____. Kurt is the _____.

A Bicycle Built for Bears, etc.

(A Bicycle Built for Bears, Teddy Bears Find a Home, Teddy Bear Totem Pole, Teddy Bear Totem Poles)

I.   **Topic Area**
Logic and problem solving.

II. **Introductory Statement**
Students will use Teddy Bear counters or other objects and higher order thinking skills to solve logic problems similar to those often encountered by the scientist.

III. **Math Skills**
a. Logical thinking
b. Problem solving
c. Inductive and deductive reasoning
d. Inferring

Science Processes
a. Comparing
b. Organizing and recording
c. Drawing conclusions
d. Inferring

IV. **Materials**
Teddy Bear counters, pictures of Teddy Bears, or other objects; crayons or colored pencils.

V.   **Key Question**
In what order are the Teddy Bears arranged?

VI. **Background Information**
The next four activities deal with arranging Teddy Bears in some order, either horizontally or vertically. Words such as ahead, between, closer, farther, above and below are used and interpreted by students.

Again, it is important to note that each statement should be studied with care and all possible inferences should be drawn from it.

The discussion in the Background Information section of Bear Soccer should be reviewed for additional information.

VII. **Management Suggestions**
See this section in Bear Soccer.

VIII. **Procedure**
See this section in Bear Soccer.

IX. **Discussion Questions**
See this section in Bear Soccer.

X.   **Analyses of Investigations**
The following discussions of how students might arrive at the solutions are only suggestive rather than exhaustive. Individual students and student groups may well have other sequences in their arguments. What is most important is that the inferences be drawn properly.

The numbers here correspond to those on the worksheets and include inferrances that may be drawn from the statements. The lettered statements are used to solve the problem.

A Bicycle Built for Bears
1. The yellow bear is removed from the "First" position.
2. The red bear is removed from the "First" and "Fourth" position since it cannot be placed there if it is between two bears.
3. The green bear is also removed from the "First" and "Fourth" position for the same reason.
   a. At this point, the only remaining possibility for the "First" position is the blue bear.
   b. The green bear must be in the third position since it is not in the fourth position (Statement 3) and the red bear separates it from the blue bear which is in the first position.
   c. Given the location of the green and blue bears, the red bear must be in the second position, leaving the yellow bear in the fourth position.
4. This statement is not necessary but provides students with another approach to solving the problem.

Teddy Bears Find a Home
1. The yellow bear cannot live in the brick house or the stucco house because it lives between two other bears. Therefore, it must live in either the wood or the stone house.

   Two arrangements are possible:
   red-yellow-green or green-yellow-red
2. The blue bear lives to the left of the red bear, closer to the grocery store.

   Therefore, the blue bear must live in the brick house since the other bears form a neighborhood "chain."

   If that is the case, the yellow bear must live in the stone house, the only remaining possibility for being between green and red.
3. By Statement 3, the yellow bear is to the left of the green bear who must then live in the stucco house; or
4. Since green and blue are not neighbors, green cannot live in the wood house and does not live in the stone house occupied by yellow and must therefore live in the stucco house.

Teddy Bear Totem Pole
First Problem: (Note: between is defined as being bounded by.)
1. The bottom bear must be red, green, or blue.
3. The green bear is not at the bottom since it is between two bears, leaving only red and blue as candidates for that position.
4. The red bear is not at the bottom since it is above the yellow bear, leaving the blue bear at the bottom.
3. The green bear is not at the top since it is between two bears leaving yellow and red as candidates for the top.

   Further, since the green bear is between yellow and blue and blue is at the bottom, green must be second from the bottom and

yellow third from the bottom; and hence red at the top.

Second Problem:

1. The red bear is not at the top and the green is not at the bottom.
2. The yellow bear is not at the top and the blue is not at the bottom.
3. The top bear is not blue. Since by 1 and 2 it is not red or yellow, it must be green.
4. The second bear from the top is red.
2. Since the blue bear is not at the bottom, the yellow bear must be at the bottom with the blue in the remaining position just above the bottom.

Teddy Bear Totem Poles

First Problem:

2,5. The yellow bears are not at the top or bottom so they must be in one of the three spaces in between.

1. Since bears of the same color cannot be next to each other the yellow bears must be second and fourth from the top.
3,4. Since the red bear is not the center (between the yellow bears) and above one of the yellow bears, it must be at the top.
1. The center and bottom are left for the blue bears and since they also cannot touch, there are two reasons why they are located in those positions.

Second Problem:

3,4. One red bear is just above the green bear and the green bear is just above the other red bear, forming a red-green-red arrangement.
5,6. Since the yellow bear is above the red-green-red arrangement and the blue bear is below, it follows that the top bear is yellow, the second is red, the third is green, the fourth is red, and the bottom is blue.

NOTE: THE TEDDY BEARS ON PAGE 35 MAY BE USED INSTEAD OF TEDDY BEAR COUNTERS.

A Bicycle Built for Bears

Name

One day, four bears went for a bicycle ride on a bicycle built for four.

1. The yellow bear was not first.
2. The red bear was between the green bear and the blue bear.
3. The green bear was between the yellow bear and the red bear.
4. The red bear is ahead of the green bear.

What position was each bear?

	First	Second	Third	Fourth
Yellow				
Red				
Blue				
Green				

Color the bears in order!

First   Second   Third   Fourth

© 1987 AIMS Education Foundation

Teddy Bears Find Home

Find out where each of these Teddy Bears lives. They are dressed in yellow, red, green, and blue.

| Grocery Store | Brick House | Wood House | Stone House | Stucco House | Fire Station |

1. The Teddy Bear dressed in yellow lives between the Teddy Bears dressed in red and green.
2. The Teddy Bear in a blue suit lives closer to the grocery store than the Teddy Bear in red dress.
3. The Teddy Bear in yellow lives farther from the fire station than the Teddy Bear in green.
4. The Teddy Bears dressed in green and blue are not neighbors.

Write a sentence to describe where each Teddy Bear lives.

1._____

2._____

3._____

4._____

Teddy Bear Totem Pole

Four Teddy Bears thought it would be fun to form a totem pole. Their colors were yellow, blue, red, and green. Here is what they noticed about their finished Teddy Bear Totem Pole.

Clues:

1. The yellow bear was not at the bottom.
2. The blue bear was not between the green bear and the red bear.
3. The green bear was between the yellow bear and the blue bear.
4. The red bear is above the yellow bear.

Build a totem pole that looks like theirs.

Bears Build Again

The four Teddy Bears built another totem pole. Their colors were yellow, blue, red, and green.

Build a totem pole to look like theirs.

Clues:

1. The red bear is somewhere below the green bear.
2. The blue bear is somewhere above the yellow bear.
3. The top bear is not blue.
4. The bear directly below the green bear is red.

Explain why you think your solution is correct.

Teddy Bear Totem Poles

Left puzzle

One red, two blue, and two yellow bears built a totem pole.

Build a totem pole like theirs.

Clues:

1. No Teddy Bears of the same color are next to each other.
2. The top Teddy Bear is not yellow.
3. The Teddy Bear in the center is not red.
4. One yellow bear is just below a red one.
5. The bottom Teddy Bear is not yellow.

Explain why you think your arrangement is correct.

Right puzzle

One blue, one green, one yellow and two red bears formed themselves into a totem pole.

Build a totem pole like theirs.

Clues:

1. The red bears are not next to each other.
2. The top bear is not red.
3. A red bear sits on the green bear.
4. The green bear sits on the red bear.
5. The yellow bear is above a red bear.
6. The blue bear is below a red bear.

Explain why your solution is correct.

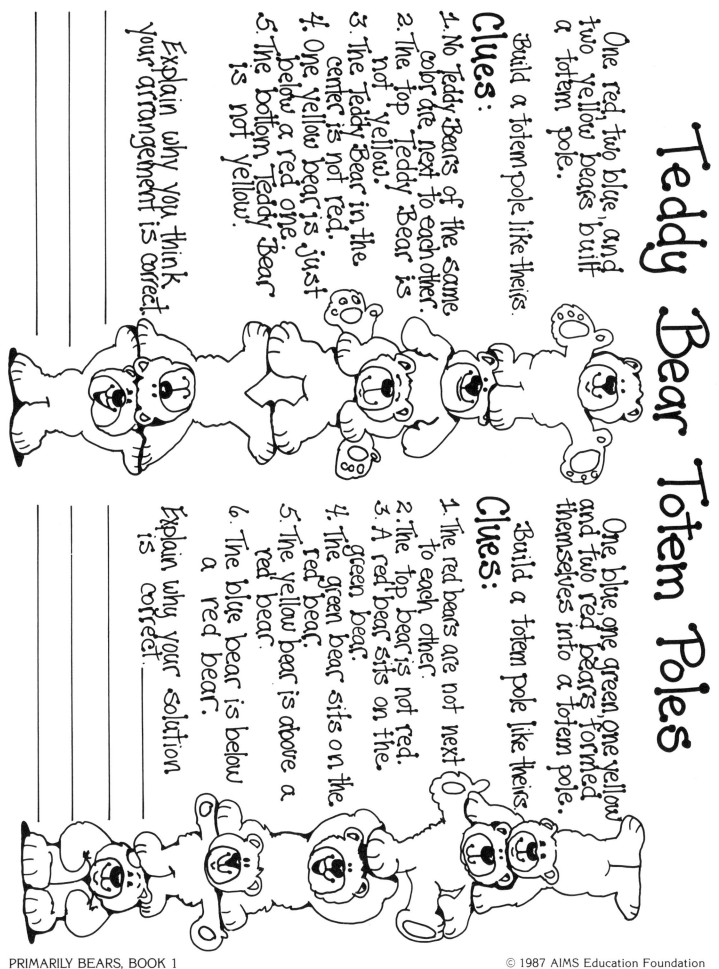

TEDDIES IN A ROW

Name:

Teddy Bears Dress for Summer, Fall Winter & Spring

I. Topic Area — Permutations

II. Introductory Statement

Students will explore an advanced mathematical idea, permutations, in a simple, gentle manner . . . describing the possible combinations of given outfits for a Teddy Bear.

III. Math Skills
a. Predicting
b. Patterning
c. Combinations
d. Comparing
e. Counting

Science Processes
a. Observing
b. Comparing
c. Recording data
d. Applying
e. Generalizing

IV. Materials

Colored pens, crayons or markers
Scissors

V. Key Question

How many different outfits can Teddy Bear make from 2 sweaters and 2 bows or from 2 hats and 2 shirts?

VI. Background Information

1. Teachers may wish to limit the combinations to include only those outfits that contain *both* a sweater *and* a bow or *both* a shirt *and* a hat. The activity may be opened for further options by allowing students to include outfits that include *only* a sweater or *only* a bow, etc.

VII. Management Suggestions

1. Discuss a random search versus an organized one. For instance, find all the outfits possible with the red shirt. Then find all the outfits with the other shirt, etc.

2. This activity may be done as a free exploration where youngsters simply picture and compare each new combination. Some, but not all, students may be able to discover and understand the generalization presented in the discussion #3.

VIII. Procedure

1. Students may color and cut out 2 sweaters and 2 bows (Fall) or the 2 shirts and 2 hats (Summer).
2. Try the outfits on the Teddy Bear pictured. Color each outfit.
3. Find a new combination and compare.
4. Record the number of different outfits for Fall, Summer, Winter and Spring.

IX. Discussion

1. How many different outfits can be made from 2 shirts and 2 hats? (4) from 2 sweaters and 2 bows? (4)
2. Draw two new articles of clothing for Teddy Bear. How many *new* combinations (using *only* new articles) can be made? (4)
3. Given 2 choices of 2 items of clothing, the number of different combinations using 2 articles, will always be _____. (4)

X. Extension

1. How many outfits could be made from 2 shirts, 2 hats and 2 pants?
($2 \times 2 \times 2 = 8$)

USE PAGES 43 AND 44 FOR MAKING A RECORD OF SOLUTIONS FOR EACH OF THE SEASONS.

Teddy Bear dresses for SUMMER!

How many different summer outfits can Teddy make from 2 hats and 2 shirts?

Color each outfit you made for Teddy.

Color and cut out.

Try the outfits on Teddy.

A

B

37

Teddy Bear dresses for FALL!

My Name

How many different fall outfits can this Teddy Bear make from 2 sweaters and 2 bows?

Color each outfit you made for Terri.

I am Terri the Teddy Bear.

© 1987 AIMS Education Foundation

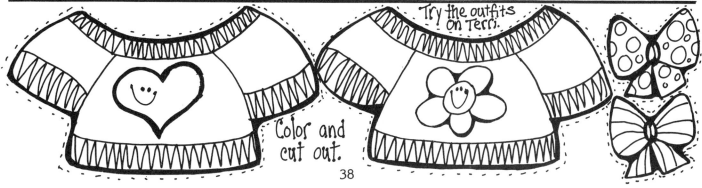

Try the outfits on Terri.

Color and cut out.

Teddy Bear Dresses for WINTER!

How many different outfits can Teddy make from 2 hats and 2 scarfs?

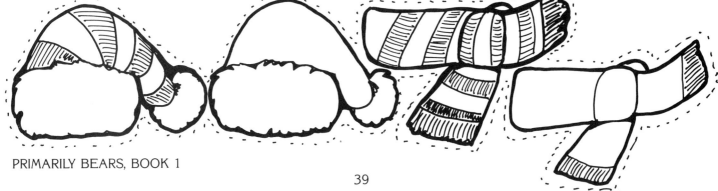

Teddy Bear Dresses for SPRING

How many different outfits can Terri Bear make from 2 skirts and 2 tops?

© 1987 AIMS Education Foundation

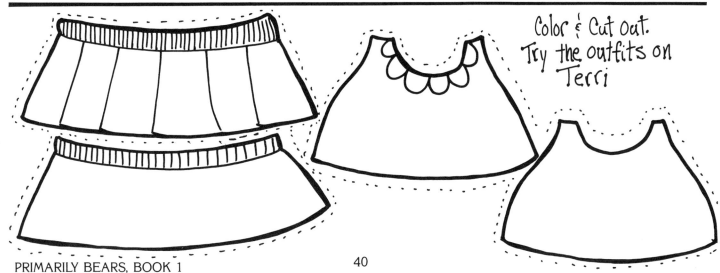

Color & Cut Out.
Try the outfits on
Terri

Terri and Teddy Bear Dress Up

I. Topic Area
A study of possible combinations.

II. Introductory Statement
Students will explore the number of different outfits Terri and Teddy Bear can make from 3 bottoms, 3 tops, and 3 objects for the head. Some students may be able to arrive at a generalization.

III. Math Skills
- a. Exploring combinations
- b. Organizing data
- c. Generalizing

Science Processes
- a. Observing
- b. Recording data
- c. Comparing
- d. Generalizing
- e. Applying

IV. Materials
- a. Terri or Teddy Bear student pages and recording pages
- b. Scissors
- c. Colored pencils or crayons

V. Key Question
How many outfits can you create for Terri (Teddy) Bear?

VI. Background Information
Combinations are used often in both mathematics and science in the study of possible interrelationships. It is important that students have both informal and formal experiences with combinations.

At the informal level students will explore the formations of different combinations, each consisting of a top, a bottom, and something placed on the head. Since there are three choices for each, there are $3 \times 3 \times 3 = 27$ possible combinations. At the informal level it is not important that students find all of the combinations.

At the formal level students may come to the generalization that the total number possible is given by the product of the individual possibilities. For example, given another situation where there were 4 tops, 2 bottoms, and 3 types of headwear, the total number of combinations would be $4 \times 2 \times 3 = 24$.

This activity provides extensive experience in making comparisons. As students record each new combination, they must compare it with all of the previous ones. As the number grows, this is an increasingly challenging task.

One way the entire class could engage in the activity would be to place each solution on the bulletin board and then challenge the students to create a new solution and explain why it is a new solution. This exercises discrimination skills.

In the case of Terri Bear, another rule may be used. Instead of dressing Terri with one of each of the objects, the following could be stated as the rule. Terri must wear one top and one bottom. But she may wear one, two, or all three objects on the head. This is possible since the bow, hat, and glasses may all be worn. If this rule is used, there are six ways in which objects could be used for the head: bow, hat, sun glasses, bow and hat, bow and sun glasses, hat and sun glasses, or all three. This means there would be 7 ways to dress the head. Therefore, there would be $3 \times 3 \times 7 = 63$ different possible outfits.

VII. Management Suggestions
This may be done as a individual, cooperative learning group, or entire class activity. The use of cooperative learning groups or the entire class as a group facilitates discussion, sharing, reasoning, and checking for differences.

VIII. Procedure
1. Determine the manner in which the students are to be organized for this investigation.
2. Explain the rules that will govern the creation of combinations.
3. Provide each student or group with a record sheet for recording the solutions, colored pencils or crayons, and scissors.
4. Ask students to cut out the various elements.
5. Have students dress the bear on the student page to compare with previously recorded solutions.
6. Determine how students will explain that a new solution has been created.
7. When a new solution has been created, instruct students to make a record of it.

IX. Discussion
1. How many different outfits can we design for Terri (Teddy) Bear?
2. If generalization has been made, pose other situations with other numbers for students to apply what they have learned.

X. Extension
Use the situation with Terri Bear where one, two, or three objects may be used on the head.

How many outfits can
Terri Bear make
from 3 bottoms,
3 tops, and
3 for her head?

shorts

tank
top

shirt

bow

hat

sun glasses

jeans

skirt

blouse

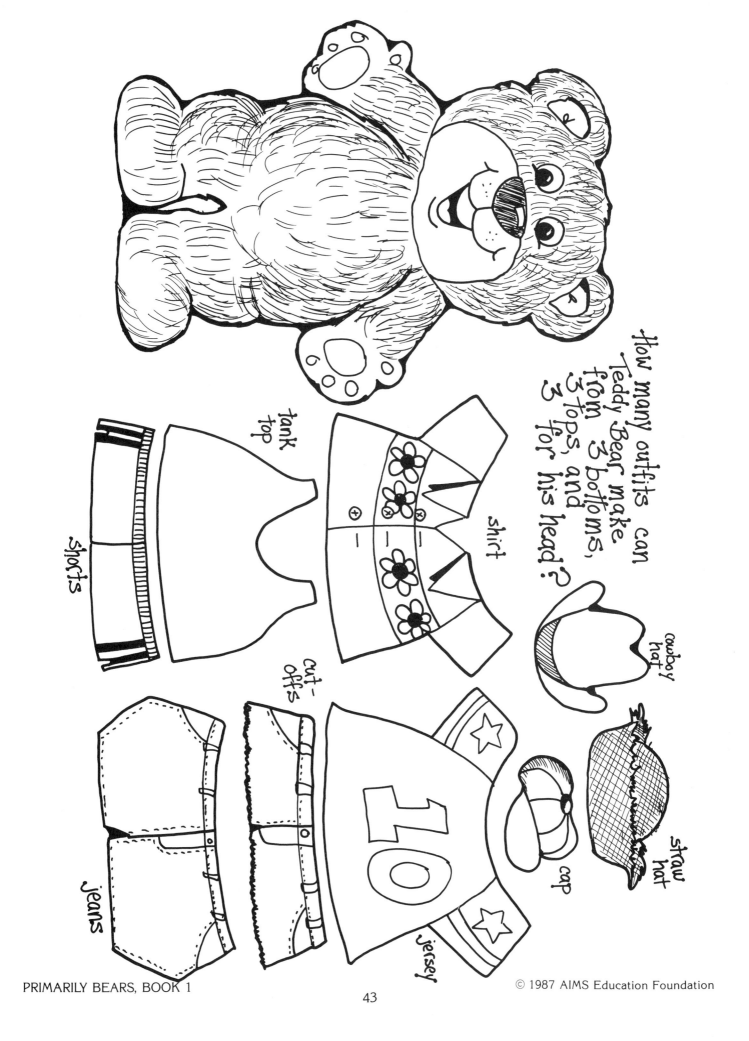

How many outfits can Teddy Bear make from 3 bottoms, 3 tops, and 3 for his head?

tank top

shorts

shirt

cut-offs

jeans

10

jersey

cowboy hat

straw hat

cap

PRIMARILY BEARS, BOOK 1

43

Make a record of the outfits you made for Terri Bear.

Make a record of the outfits you made for Teddy Bear.

The Teddy Bears Go Sledding

I. Topic Area
Patterns, arrangements (permutations), and problem solving.

II. Introductory Statement
Students will explore arrangements or permutations involving 2, 3, and 4 objects to create a pattern for predicting a general result.

III. Math Skills
a. Forming arrangements
b. Studying patterns
c. Generalizing

Science Processes
a. Organizing data
b. Drawing conclusions
c. Hypothesizing
d. Predicting

IV. Materials
4 Teddy Bears of different colors.
A sheet of paper for listing all of the possible arrangments.

V. Key Question
In how many ways could 2, 3, or 4 people arrange themselves on a sled?

VI. Background Information
The number of arrangements or permutations with n objects is n!

For example, the number of arrangements of 2 objects is 2! or 2 x 1 = 2.

The number of arrangements of 3 objects is 3! or 3 x 2 x 1 = 6.

The number of arrangements of 4 objects is 4! or 4 x 3 x 2 x 1 = 24.

Obviously, the number increases rapidly since 5! = 120 and 6! = 720, etc.

VII. Management Suggestions
Students may work individually or in cooperative learning groups. They should share their results by comparing individual arrangements. Students could be encouraged to find a systematic way of making sure they have all of the arangements.

VIII. Procedure
1. Have students find all possible arrangements for two objects, in this case two Teddy Bears on a sled, and record it in the table.

2. Next, have students find all possible arrangements of three Teddy Bears. Since there are six cases this will be a challenge for some students. Enter the result in the table.

3. Have students find the arrangements possible with four objects. This will challenge all of the students. If some students have found a systematic way of doing this, have them share this with the class.

4. Introduce students to the notion of factorial notation. Lead them to discover the general result.

IX. Discussion
1. What do expressions such as 7! mean?
2. In how many ways could 8 people arrange themselves in a row for a picture?

The TEDDY BEARS Go Sledding

1. Two Teddy Bears are trying to decide how they should arrange themselves on a sled. One has a yellow suit and the other a red one. Help them find all the possible ways.

Front Seat	Back Seat
yellow	
red	

2. A third Teddy Bear dressed in a blue suit joins them. Now, in how many ways can they arrange themselves on a sled?

Front	Center	Back
yellow		
yellow		
red		
red		
blue		
blue		

3. Later, a fourth Teddy Bear dressed in a green suit joins the first three. In how many ways can 4 Teddy Bears arrange themselves on the sled? Design your own chart below.

4. Place the gathered information into this table. Look for a pattern.

Number of Teddy Bears	Number of Arrangements
Two	
Three	
Four	

5. CHALLENGE! How many ways would 5 Teddy Bears arrange themselves on the sled?

Teddy Bears Playing In The Den

I. Topic Area
The use of random samples to make predictions about a population.

II. Introductory Statement
Students will investigate random samples to determine how they can be used to make predictions about the nature of a population. In both science and mathematics, generalizations are frequently drawn from random samples.

III. Math Skills
a. Random sampling
b. Classifying and counting
c. Entering information into a table
d. Ordering
e. Writing mathematical sentences
f. Adding
g. Constructing a circle graph

Science Processes
a. Classifying
b. Organizing data
c. Drawing conclusions
d. Generalizing
e. Hypothesizing
f. Predicting
g. Comparing

IV. Materials
24 Teddy Bears or other objects divisible into four categories for each group.
A container such as a box for each group.

V. Key Question
Can we predict how many Teddy Bears there are of each color from drawing random samples?

VI. Background Information
Random samples are used extensively in our society to form the basis for drawing conclusions. Quality control in many industries consists of taking random samples and subjecting them to tests. **Consumers Report,** for example, continually tests random samples to determine the quality of products. New drugs are tested in a similar manner. Political pollsters use random sampling as the basis for their projections.

A random sample is one in which no bias occurs in the selection of the sample. The entire group is known as the population. So, we make a prediction about the population from a random sample or samples.

VII. Management Suggestions
Organize the students into cooperative learning groups. Encourage the groups to discuss their conclusions and arrive at their best group predictions.

VIII. Procedure
1. Organize students into cooperative learning groups.
2. Supply each group with 24 Teddy Bears of assorted colors with one color predominant and another deficient. Also, provide each group with a container in which to hide the Teddy Bears.
3. Students will thoroughly mix the Teddy Bears without looking into the container and then draw out six for each sample at random. Be sure to emphasize the nature and requirement of a random selection.
4. As each sample is drawn, students will classify them, count each sub-group and enter the information in the table. The sample will then be returned to the container and thoroughly mixed with the rest of the population.
5. After the total of each color is determined for the four samples, the group should discuss what their prediction about the 24 Teddy Bears should be and enter that into the table.
6. The distribution should then be graphed in the "prediction" rim of the circle graph.
7. Students will next empty the entire population out of the box and classify the Teddy Bears.
8. Students will enter the information in the table and compare it with their predictions.
9. The Teddy Bears will then be placed into the indicated regions in the outer rim of the circle graph to form a three-dimensional circle graph.
10. The students will visually compare their prediction and the population using the graph.
11. Students will complete the final page, writing statements and mathematical sentences.

IX. Discussion
1. What is a random sample? A population?
2. How accurately could we predict from the random samples?
3. Why is it important to thoroughly mix the Teddy Bears before a sample is drawn?
4. Why should the drawing be made without looking?
5. Where are random samples used?

X. Extensions
1. Try other sampling configurations using samples of other sizes with populations of other sizes.
2. Have students develop a sampling activity such as taking a pool from a sample and predicting it onto a population.
3. If the school has a hot lunch program, have students use the information as to the number in the classroom participating each day of the week to predict the number from the school participating.
4. Have the students gather newspaper articles that are based on predicting on the basis of a sample.

PRIMARILY BEARS, BOOK 1

© 1987 AIMS Education Foundation

TEDDY BEARS
Playing in the Den

1. 24 Teddy Bears are playing a game in their den. They are hidden from view. Every little while, 6 are sent out while the rest lay their plans in secret. The 6 who come out are selected at random. Some have been sent out before, some are sent out for the first time.

Your task is to make the best guess as to how many Teddy Bears there are of each color.

My Guess

1. I think there will be more _____ Teddy Bears than any other color.
2. I think there will be fewer _____ Teddy Bears than any other color.

2. Pick out 6 Teddy Bears for each sample without looking into the den (box). After the number of Teddy Bears of each color in the sample has been recorded, put them back into the den, mix them up thoroughly, and pick 6 more until 4 samples have been checked.

	Blue	Red	Green	Yellow
First Sample				
Second Sample				
Third Sample				
Fourth Sample				
Total in all Samples				

3. From this information, predict how many there actually are of each color. Graph this on the circle graph. Then bring all the Teddy Bears out of the den and count the number of each color. Compare the actual with your prediction.

	Blue	Red	Green	Yellow
My Prediction				
The Actual Number				

4. The colors of the Teddy Bears arranged from most to least is:

_____ , _____ , _____ , _____
most   least

Graph your predictions for the number of Teddy Bears of each color. Use the order of blue, red, green, and yellow beginning at "12 o'clock". Use the same colors as the Teddy Bears.

Next, place the Teddy Bears on the outside rim of your circle graph to form a real "Teddy Bear Graph". Use the same color order of blue, red, green, and yellow, also beginning at "12 o'clock."

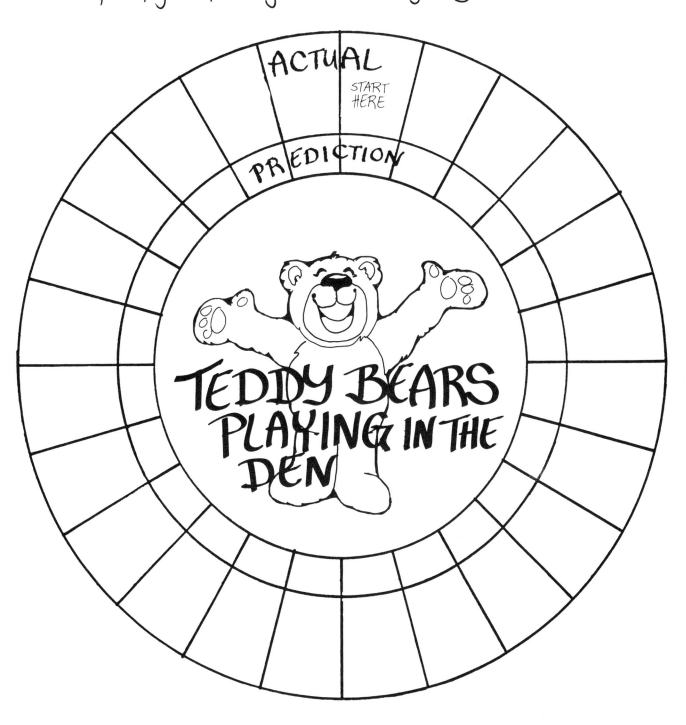

ACTUAL

START HERE

PREDICTION

TEDDY BEARS PLAYING IN THE DEN

TEDDY BEARS
Playing in the Den

Name _____

1. Compare your prediction with the actual result. _____
_____

2. Complete 4 different sentences from your investigation, each in two ways. Use the names of colors in the first, and numbers in the second.

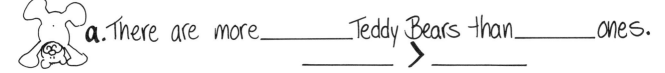

a. There are more _____ Teddy Bears than _____ ones.

_____ > _____

b. There are more _____ Teddy Bears than _____ ones.

_____ > _____

c. There are fewer _____ Teddy Bears than _____ ones.

_____ < _____

d. There are fewer _____ Teddy Bears than _____ ones.

_____ < _____

3. Which sample is most like the actual result? _____
_____

4. Are 4 samples better than just one sample? Explain: _____
_____
_____

5. Complete these sentences from the result of the full set of 24 bears.

a. _____ + _____ = _____   c. _____ + _____ = _____
   red   blue   green   yellow

b. _____ + _____ = _____   d. _____ + _____ = _____
   green   red   yellow blue

PRIMARILY BEARS, BOOK 1

51

© 1987 AIMS Education Foundation

Teddy Bear Clubs Go Weighing

Topic
Mass measurement

Key Question
What is the fewest number of clubs you can use to find the mass of objects?

Focus
Student will find the masses of a variety of objects in a problem-solving mode using mass sets based on base two numbers.

Guiding Documents
Project 2061 Benchmark
- *Numbers can be used to count things, place them in order, or name them.*

NRC Standards
- *Employ simple equipment and tools to gather data and extend the senses.*
- *Objects have many observable properties, including size, weight, shape, color, temperature, and the ability to react with other substances. Those properties can be measured using tools, such as rulers, balances, and thermometers.*

NCTM Standards
- *Make and use estimates of measurement*
- *Make and use measurements in problems and everyday situations*
- *Apply estimation in working with quantities, measurement, computation, and problem solving*
- *Relate physical materials, pictures, and diagrams to mathematical ideas*

Math
Measurement
   mass
Problem solving
Basic operations
   addition
Graphing

Integrated Processes
Observing
Comparing and contrasting
Collecting and recording data
Generalizing

Materials
Teddy Bear Counters
Balances
Various objects (see *Management 2*)
Crayons or markers: red, green, yellow, blue

Background Information
This is an investigation involving finding the mass of various objects but with a different twist: using the fewest number of "clubs."

The number of members in the clubs is based on the place value of base two numbers: 8, 4, 2, 1 in that order. This is the numeration system that underlies all computer languages. It is not necessary for students to know this, but for some it might be of interest. Nevertheless, that knowledge is not necessary for the investigation

All possible unit masses from 1 to 15 have a unique solution. As examples, an object with a mass of 7 Teddy Bears will be balanced only by the green (4 bear members), yellow (2 bear members), and blue (1 bear member) clubs; an object with a mass of 12 will be balanced only by the red (8 bear members) and green (4 bear members) clubs; and an object with a mass of 14 will be balanced only by the red (8 bear members), green (4 bear members), and yellow (2 bear members) clubs. *Only one club of each color is used in each situation.*

Students will engage in problem solving as they use trial and error at the outset to balance an object. In time, they may well use more advanced reasoning. As they build the graph they will have a visual basis for making generalizations.

Management
1. This activity is most effective with collaborative groups of three to four students.
2. The objects should be carefully selected beforehand. Each set of objects should contain those that have a mass very close to a given number of Teddy Bear Counters. Masses of 5, 6, 7, 8, 9, 10, 11, 12, 13, 14, and 15 Teddy Bear Counters provide interesting challenges. The objects can be pencils of various lengths, clay balls, bags of beans, and other objects which have the desired mass or which can be readily increased or decreased in mass to equal one of the desired masses.
3. Each group of students should have the following set of Teddy Bear clubs: 8 red bears, 4 green bears, 2 yellow bears, and 1 blue bear.
4. If students have a difficult time remembering that the entire club (number of members is determined by color) must be used, you may want to wrap each club is a small piece of plastic wrap so that the entire club must move together.

Procedure
1. Provide each group with the necessary materials: balances, Teddy Bear clubs, and collected objects.
2. Inform students that all bears of one color must be used at the same time; they are not to break up the clubs.

3. It may be best to model the procedure by selecting one object and showing how to use the clubs to find its mass. Demonstrate how to fill in the information on the first student page.

4. Have students follow the procedure for the set of objects they have been given. Direct them to enter the information into the table, naming the object, recording the colors of the clubs, and listing the number of members of each club used. In the third column only the appropriate number of addends will be entered and this will generally be less than four. The total number of bears is then recorded in the last column.

5. Have students complete the graph on the second page. They must use the fewest number of clubs possible. The pattern becomes most obvious when students are instructed to use the largest club first, then the next largest, etc. Depending on the age and ability of the group, this may best be done as a whole class experience, or you may want to do several examples to get the students started.

Discussion

1. Did you notice any pattern in the number and type of clubs used? Explain.

2. Did you notice any pattern in the graph? Explain.

3. Were you able to find the mass of all the objects? Why do you think this was possible? [The combinations of 8, 4, 2, and 1 could be used for any object with a mass from 1 Teddy Bear Counter to 15 Teddy Bear Counters. (1, 2, 2 + 1 = 3, 4, 4 + 1 = 5, 4 + 2 = 6, 4 + 2 + 1 = 7, 8, 8 + 1 = 9, 8 + 2 = 10, 8 + 2 + 1 = 11, 8 + 4 = 12, 8 + 4 + 1 = 13, 8 + 4 + 2 = 14, 8 + 4 + 2 + 1 = 15)]

4. If we wanted to find the mass of heavier objects, how many bears should be in the fifth club? [16] ... sixth club? [32]

Teddy Bear Clubs Go Weighing

These Teddy Bear clubs have this many members:

Red   = 8 bears
Green = 4 bears
Yellow = 2 bears
Blue   = 1 bear

The members of each club are very good friends and always go weighing together. For example, if one red bear is to be used to find the mass of an object, all eight red bears must be used. The same is true for each of the other clubs.

In the following, find out which club or combination of clubs are used to find the mass of each object.

Object	Color of Club or Clubs Needed to Balance	List of Number in Each Club Used	Total Number of Bears
		___ + ___ + ___ + ___ =	
		___ + ___ + ___ + ___ =	
		___ + ___ + ___ + ___ =	
		___ + ___ + ___ + ___ =	
		___ + ___ + ___ + ___ =	
		___ + ___ + ___ + ___ =	
		___ + ___ + ___ + ___ =	
		___ + ___ + ___ + ___ =	

 Teddy Bear Clubs Make Graphs

The Teddy Bear clubs have this many members:

Red   = 8 bears
Green = 4 bears
Yellow = 2 bears
Blue   = 1 bear

These Teddy Bear clubs like to be used in graphs. Show which club or clubs would be used to make these totals. If any member of the club is used, all the members must be used. Use the colors of the clubs in your graph.

Total Number
of Bears

1
2
3
4
5
6
7
8
9
10
11
12
13
14
15

54

Topic
Finding the mass of oranges in non-standard units.

Key Question
What is the mass of your orange in Teddy Bears?

Focus
Students will use a non-standard unit of measure, Teddy Bears, to count, to find mass, and to compare.

Guiding Documents
Project 2061 Benchmark
- *Numbers can be used to count things, place them in order, or name them.*

NRC Standards
- *Employ simple equipment and tools to gather data and extend the senses.*
- *Objects have many observable properties, including size, weight, shape, color, temperature, and the ability to react with other substances. Those properties can be measured using tools, such as rulers, balances, and thermometers.*

NCTM Standards
- *Make and use estimates of measurement*
- *Make and use measurements in problems and everyday situations*
- *Apply estimation in working with quantities, measurement, computation, and problem solving*
- *Relate physical materials, pictures, and diagrams to mathematical ideas*

Math
Counting
Measuring
 mass
Estimating
Adding and subtracting
Writing equations

Integrated Processes
Observing
Comparing
Recording data
Communicating

Materials
For the class:
 oranges, one for each group
 balances
 Teddy Bear Counters

Background Information
To build a strong foundation in the concept of measurement, children need many experiences with non-standard units of measurement. By using Teddy Bear Counters, the activity becomes a simple counting experience. Teddy Bear Counters come in four colors: red, yellow, blue and green and lend themselves well for many counting, measuring, comparing, and patterning activities.

Management
1. Oranges tend to be messy but one can limit the mess by scoring the orange rind into crescent shaped sections to facilitate peeling.
2. One may wish to substitute tangerines for oranges. Their mass is less and they are easier to peel.
3. Choose small oranges. If the oranges are too heavy, the number of Teddy Bears necessary to balance their mass may be unwieldy.

Procedure
1. Ask the students to guess how many Teddy Bears it takes to balance their oranges. Have them record this estimate.
2. Direct them to put the orange in the balance. Instruct the students to put in enough Teddy Bears to balance the orange, making certain that the pans of the balance are even. Have them record the number of red, yellow, green, and blue Teddy Bears it took to balance the orange. Then have them find how many there are all together.
3. Ask the students to compare their guesses to the actual number of Teddy Bears it took to balance the orange.
4. Peel the oranges. Have the students estimate the mass of the peeling in Teddy Bears Counters. Make sure they record their estimates.
5. Have them find and record the mass of the peeling in Teddy Bear Counters.
6. Challenge the students to estimate how many Teddy Bears it takes to equal the mass of the eating part (pulp) of the orange. Have them find the mass, count, and record the results.

7. Distribute the last student page and ask students to tell the story in their own words. "First, I guessed...."

Discussion

1. Let's write a number story about your orange. Let the letter "O" stand for the whole orange. Let "P" stand for the peeling and "E" for the eating part. The whole orange, O, is equal to the sum of the parts, P and E, or O = P + E. Substitute appropriate numbers in the equation. In some cases, the parts may have a mass that is greater than the whole because the Teddy Bears are not a critical enough measuring tool and students are measuring to the nearest Teddy Bear. Furthermore, measurement is always approximate, not exact. Some students may recognize the problem and tell you that the peeling for instance has a mass of 14 1/2 Teddy Bears when they know halves.

2. Now, write a subtraction number story. If I have the whole orange, O, and I eat the eating part, E, how much do I have left? 0 - E = P.

3. Let students use the Teddy Bears to retell the story and show that the whole is equal to the sum of its parts or that when you remove or take away one of the parts, the other part is leftover.

Extension

Try other fruits. Build the concepts of whole = part + part and whole - part = part

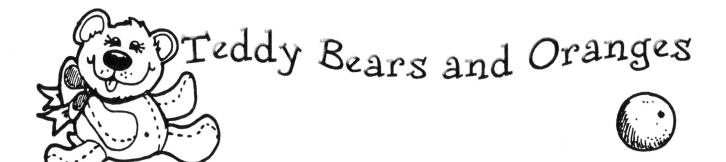

Teddy Bears and Oranges

I think the mass of my orange will be

_____ Teddy Bears.

How many Teddy Bears are there?

Reds _____   Greens _____

Yellows _____   Blues _____

The mass of the whole orange is

_____ Teddy Bears.

My guess was _____ Teddy Bears too high.

My guess was _____ Teddy Bears too low

Teddy Bears and Oranges

I think the mass of my orange peel will be ____ Teddy Bears.

How many Teddy Bears are there?

Reds _____   Greens _____

Yellows _____   Blues _____

The mass of the orange peel is

_____ Teddy Bears.

My guess was _____ Teddy Bears too high.

My guess was _____ Teddy Bears too low

Teddy Bears and Oranges

I think the mass of eating part will be _____ Teddy Bears.

How many Teddy Bears are there?

Reds _____   Greens _____

Yellows _____   Blues _____

The mass of the eating part is

_____ Teddy Bears.

My guess was _____ Teddy Bears too high.

My guess was _____ Teddy Bears too low

Teddy Bears and Oranges

The mass of the peeling part is _____ Teddy Bears.

The mass of the eating part is _____ Teddy Bears.

The mass of the whole orange is _____ Teddy Bears.

The peeling + The eating part = The whole orange

_____ + _____ = _____

Teddy Bears and Oranges

Now you tell the story:

I guessed that the mass of the whole orange
_____

would be _____

_____

- -

_____

- -

_____

- -

_____

- -

_____

- -

_____

- -

_____

_____

- -

_____

Gummy Bears

I. Topic Area
Number Concepts and Graphing.

II. Introductory Statement
Students will use Gummy Bears to count, classify and construct a graph.

III. Math Skills
  a. Estimating
  b. Counting
  c. Comparing
  d. Computation
  e. Graphing
  f. Problem solving

Science Processes
  a. Observing
  b. Classifying
  c. Recording data
  d. Communicating
  e. Using knowledge to solve problems

IV. Materials
Assortment of Gummy Bears randomly portioned into small Ziploc baggies—approximately 10-15 per baggie.

V. Key Question
How many Gummy Bears are in your baggie?

VI. Background Information
Gummy Bears may be purchased by the pound (bulk) or by the bag. Randomly select a number of Gummy Bears for each baggie making sure the number is appropriate for the grade level. (10-12 for very primary grades—more for others.)

VII. Management Suggestions
In making comparisons of sets of bears, the teacher may ask appropriate questions, but also allow time for students to observe and share comparisons of their own.

VIII. Procedure
1. Distribute a small baggie of Gummy Bears to each small group of students.
2. Have students estimate how many bears are in a baggie.
3. Record estimates on chalkboard or overhead. Ask questions about the estimates listed. Do you see your age? Can you find a number that is the same as 4 + 3, 10 − 2, or 3 more than 9, etc.
4. Sort bears according to color on sorting sheet.
5. Make a record of the number of bears on sorting sheet.
6. Build a real graph of bears by forming columns of bears in each color—placing one bear in each square. Which color has the most? the least?
7. Make a representational graph by coloring the pictures of the bears and placing a picture in each square as you remove each Gummy Bear.
8. In the large Gummy Bear pattern draw or write a number story about Gummy Bears. For example, three red Gummy Bears and four white Gummy Bears make seven Gummy Bears altogether.

IX. Discussion
1. Discussion will vary at the discretion of the teacher. Suggested ideas include: adding or subtracting the sets by color; comparing sets by using relationship signs ($<$, $>$, $=$).

X. Extension
1. Use Gummy Bears to make pattern strips where students observe and recognize the pattern and then complete or repeat it.

Gummy Bears
Sorting Sheet

red

orange

white

yellow

green

Name:_____

Gummy Bears Tally

I had _____ yellow s.

I had _____ orange s.

I had _____ red s.

I had _____ white s.

I had _____ green s.

I had _____ s in all.

yellow	orange	red	white	green

Name:

| yellow | orange | red | white | green |

Gummy
Bear
Pattern

© 1987 AIMS Education Foundation

MATH WITH "M&M'S" ® CANDIES

Topic
Process skills and collaborative learning

Key Questions
1. How many candies are there in one bag?
2. The color with the greatest number of candies is _____?
3. The color with the fewest number of candies is_____?

Focus
In this activity the students will estimate the number of "M&M's"® candies, and complete the activities of addition and subtraction. Students will also be asked to use letters to represent the colors of candies and perform operations of addition and subtraction or state relationships.

Math
Counting
Addition
Subtraction
Graphing

Integrated Processes
Observing
Comparing and contrasting
Classifying
Gathering and recording data
Interpreting data

Materials
For each group:
   one bag of plain "M&M's"® candies
   colored pencils, markers, or crayons

Management
1. Have the class work in groups of three or four pupils.
2. Assign a task to each child in the group:
   a. A RECORDER to write the number of each color of candies, and to record answers.
   b. A SORTER to separate the candies into colors.
   c. A GRAPHER to prepare a picture or bar graph the number of candies in the group's bag.
3. You may want each child to complete the questions 1 through 10, or you may want each trio to turn in one completed paper for their group. If you do this, remember that each child's name should be on the completed activity sheets and be able to tell or report just what happened in each part of the activity.

4. This activity should take approximately 40 minutes. You may want to extend this activity to another period of time with the whole class preparing whole class records, graphs, and predicting the number of candies that each group has.

Procedure
1. Assign the students to collaborative learning groups. You may do this by having the children "count off" by tens. If you have 30 children in your class—all of the ones form a group, etc. until all of the children are in a group.
2. Have children move to their groups. Explain that each group will be working together as a team and that they will complete their activity together. At this point, it would be good for them to receive the four activity sheets. Pass out one set of four activity sheets for the group. Explain that each person will have a very important job to perform for the group.
   a. The SORTER will open the bag of candies (remember that you have not passed out the bags of candies yet) and sort them by colors. Have SORTER hold up the activity sheet that has the seven circles with colors printed in the centers—red, orange, green, yellow, blue, dark brown, and one empty set—so that everyone knows what sheet is being used and so that each SORTER knows his/her job.
   b. The RECORDER is to work with the two activity sheets with the numerals 1-11 on them. Have the RECORDER show these two activity sheets. He/she will record the number of candies by color and will be assisted by others in the group; especially the SORTER. All three members of the group are to confirm that they know how many of each color of candies there are in the bag.
   c. The GRAPHER is to work with the single activity sheet that shows spaces for each color in five columns; have each GRAPHER show this activity sheet. GRAPHERS can prepare bar graphs by extending each column with additional paper glued to the top of the activity sheet. The GRAPHER can also prepare a chart showing the number of candies for each color by drawing small circles in each column.
3. Next pass out the candy bags (one bag to each group). Have each student begin his/her task in the activity. If each child is doing individual activity sheets, be certain that all the information is recorded on each of the activity sheets.

4. Be certain that the students know what each of the symbols mean on the activity sheet.
   G represents green colored candies
   R represents red colored candies
   B represents blue colored candies
   O represents orange colored candies
   Y represents yellow colored candies
   DB represents dark brown colored candies
   > means greater than
   < means less than
   = means equal
   B & DB means the number of blue candies plus the number of dark brown candies equals_____.
5. Remember that each student is part of the learning group and that the candies can be used to actually count and solve the problems. Allow the students to manipulate the candies and check each others problems.
6. In doing problem number 8, please make certain that each student has 15 candies and that the left-overs are set aside or placed in a container until the activity is completed. This part of the activity is an excellent place for cooperation to take place and confirmation of right answers to happen. Encourage each child in the group to do his/her part.

7. Complete the graph and post the results from each group.

Discussion

1. Do all of the candy bags used in this activity contain the same number of candies? How can you explain this?
2. Which color had the most candies?
3. Why do you think that there were more dark brown candies in the bag?
4. What combination of two colors produce the greatest amount of candies?
5. How does the number of dark brown candies compare with the number of all of the other candies together?

Extensions

1. There are other products that can be substituted for "M&M"s"® candies, such as cookies, crackers, breakfast cereals and other candies (jelly beans).
2. Prepare different types of graphs—picture graphs and bar graphs.
3. Prepare graphs of other types of activities in the classroom—ages, birth months, favorite pets, or favorite books.

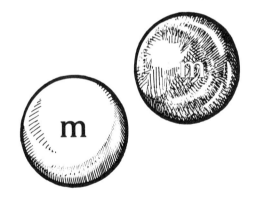

Name_____

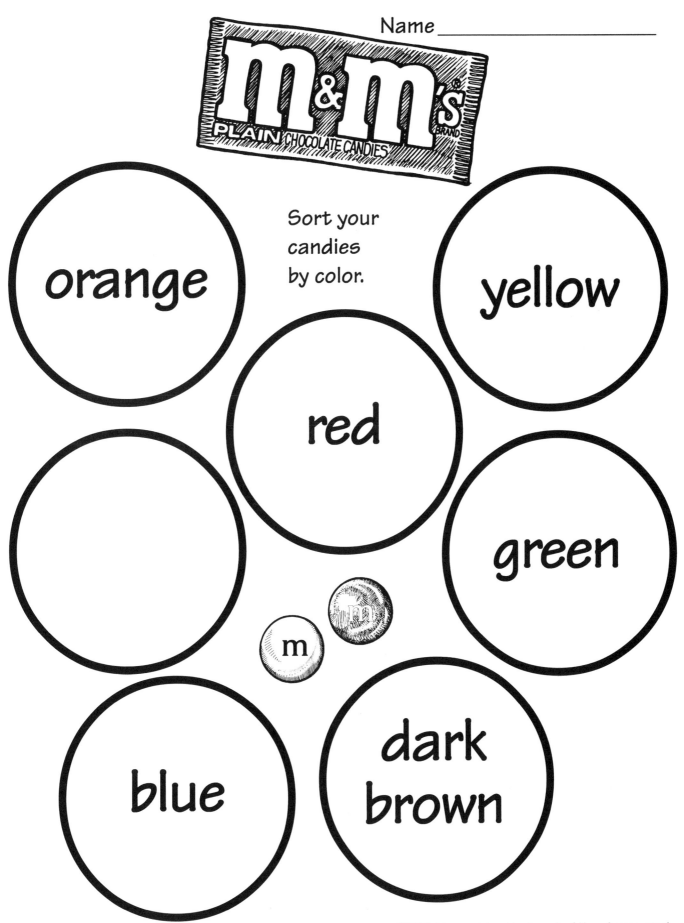

Sort your candies by color.

orange

yellow

red

green

blue

dark brown

67

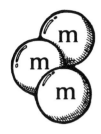 

Math

1. Do not open your bag yet. Guess how many of the candies are in your bag. _____

2. Open your bag, and count the candies. How many candies are in the bag? _____

3. How far off was your guess? _____

4. Now put your candies into sets by color.

( ) green = G   ( ) red = R   ( ) blue = B

( ) orange = O   ( ) yellow = Y   ( ) dark brown = DB

5. Write the number of candies in each set.

set G = _____   set R = _____   set B = _____

set O = _____   set Y = _____   set DB = _____

6. Using > or < or =, show the relationship between these sets.

G _____ R   Y _____ DB   Y _____ B

O _____ G   DB _____ B   G _____ Y

G _____ B   Y _____ R   G _____ DB

7. Do these problems:

B + DB = _____   O + G = _____   O + B = _____

R + O = _____   R + Y = _____   G + B = _____

R + G = _____   Y + B = _____

8. Put 15 candies in a pile in front of you. Use them to do these problems.

   How many piles of four can you make? _____

      How many are left? _____

   How many piles of seven can you make? _____

      How many are left? _____

   How many piles of five can you make? _____

      How many are left? _____

   How many piles of two can you make? _____

      How many are left? _____

9. Put two of the candies in your mouth.

      How many are left ? _____

10. Eat four more.

      How many candies do you have left now? _____

11. Do what you wish with the rest of your candies: eat them now, save them, take them home OR hold them in your hand and see if they melt!!!

Have fun and have a great day!!

Name _____

"m&m's" Math

Dark Brown	Green	Orange	Yellow	Red	Blue

"M&M's" is a registered trademark of Mars, Incorporated

© 2000 AIMS Education Foundation

The Joys of Jelly Beans

I. Topic Area
Science process skills and jelly beans.

II. Introductory Statement
Students will use jelly beans to estimate, count, compare and graph.

III. Math Skills
a. Estimating
b. Counting
c. Comparing
d. Graphing
e. Column addition

Science Processes
a. Sorting & classifying
b. Hypothesizing
c. Recording data
d. Generalizing
e. Using information to solve problems

IV. Materials
Jelly beans
Crayons or colored pencils

V. Key Question
How many jelly beans are in the jar?

VI. Background Information
The teacher may wish to purchase one large bag of jelly beans and find an appropriately decorative jar in which to display them. Perhaps an old fashioned canning jar or an apothecary jar through which students may view the full assortment of candy would be available.

VII. Procedure
1. The teacher will display the jar of jelly beans and initiate a sharing time during which students are encouraged to voice their estimates as to how many jelly beans are in the jar. The teacher records these estimates on the chalk board or overhead projector.

2. A discussion of the shared answers may then ensue as the teacher asks creative questions while the students observe the numbers on the overhead. Such questions may include: Who sees a number that is the same as their age? Is there a number with a 3 in the tens place? Do you see a number that is the same as 5 plus 4? The questions will vary in complexity according to the grade level ability.

3. The teacher will then distribute to each small group of 4-5 students a small handful or baggie of the jelly beans removed from the jar until all jelly beans are distributed.

She (or he) may point out that the job of counting all the jelly beans becomes much easier when shared in small portions.

4. Each student then estimates or guesses the total number of jelly beans in their fistful and the number of each color and makes a record on the student activity page.

5. Each group then counts the jelly beans and sorts by color on his sorting sheet. Record the total count and the number of each color.

6. Each student then makes a graph of the number and colors of jelly beans in his group. Either the horizontal bar graph or the vertical bar graph may be used. In either situation, a real graph may be constructed first by placing the jelly beans directly on the page - one to a square or one to an oval. A representational graph may be drawn by having each student simply color in each space as they remove each jelly bean from the paper.

7. In order to discover the total number of all the jelly beans in the jar students will share the information from each group and the teacher may use the vertical graph in a transparency form and record the number of each color in the appropriate columns. Thus, the red column may show a column of numbers such as 5, 4, 3, etc. Vertically the total number of each color in the jar will be displayed. Horizontally the numbers will total the number of jelly beans in each small group.

VIII. Discussion Questions
1. Let's compare our estimates to the actual count in the jar. How many of you were within ten of the number? five?
2. Which color jelly bean was the most common?
3. How are the jelly beans alike and how are they different?
4. Why do you suppose that jelly beans often appear in Easter baskets?
5. How many "counting Teddy Bears" did our jar of jelly beans weight?
6. Choose jelly beans of two colors. Make a jelly bean "train" that shows a repeating pattern. Try it again with three different colors.
7. Fair share the jelly beans in your group with the members of your team. How many did each person get? How many are left over?

PRIMARILY BEARS, BOOK 1

Name _____

JELLY BEANS

My guess _____

The Easter Bunny just hopped by
  And left these jelly beans in our jar!
Before you begin to count them,
  Try to guess how many there are!

Quickly, come up with your answer
  And write it on the lid.
Now count up all the beans
  To see how well you did!

© 1987 AIMS Education Foundation

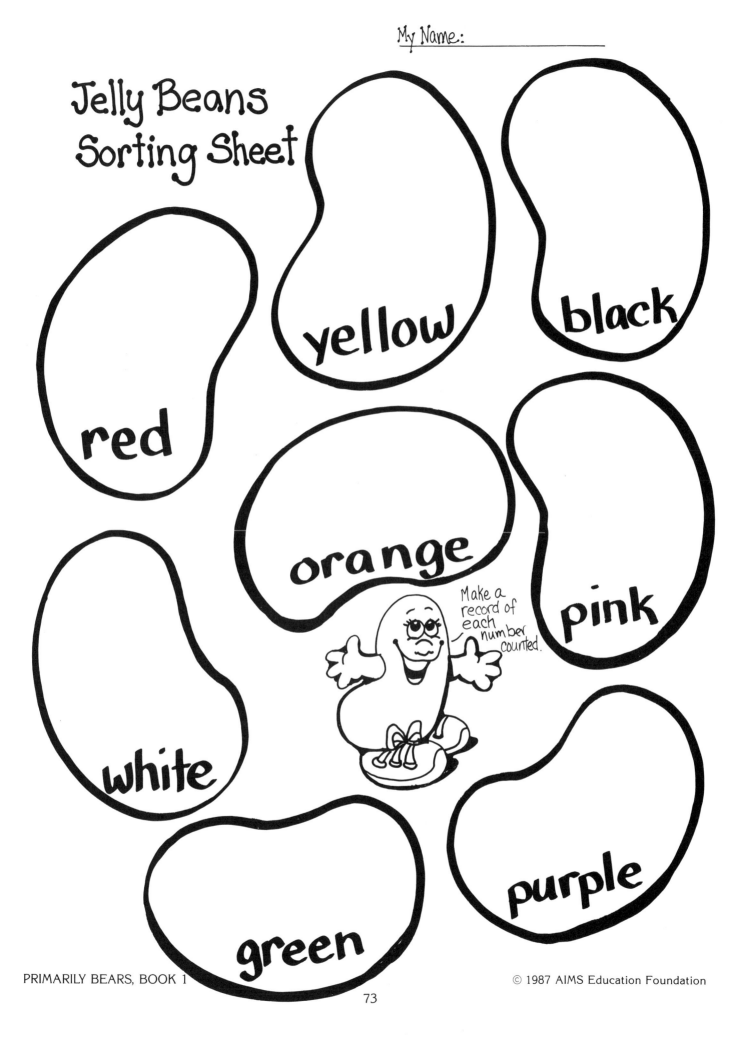

JELLY BEANS

My group got a bag of jelly beans.

Our bag cost_____and weighed_____.

I guessed that there were this many:

_____ red ◯'s
_____ orange ◯'s
_____ yellow ◯'s
_____ green ◯'s
_____ purple ◯'s
_____ pink ◯'s
_____ white ◯'s
+ _____ black ◯'s
_____ total ◯'s

My group counted this many:

_____ red ◯'s
_____ orange ◯'s
_____ yellow ◯'s
_____ green ◯'s
_____ purple ◯'s
_____ pink ◯'s
_____ white ◯'s
+ _____ black ◯'s
_____ total ◯'s

PRIMARILY BEARS, BOOK 1

© 1987 AIMS Education Foundation

Name _____

Jelly Beans

10
9
8
7
6
5
4
3
2
1
0

red | orange | yellow | green | purple | pink | white | black

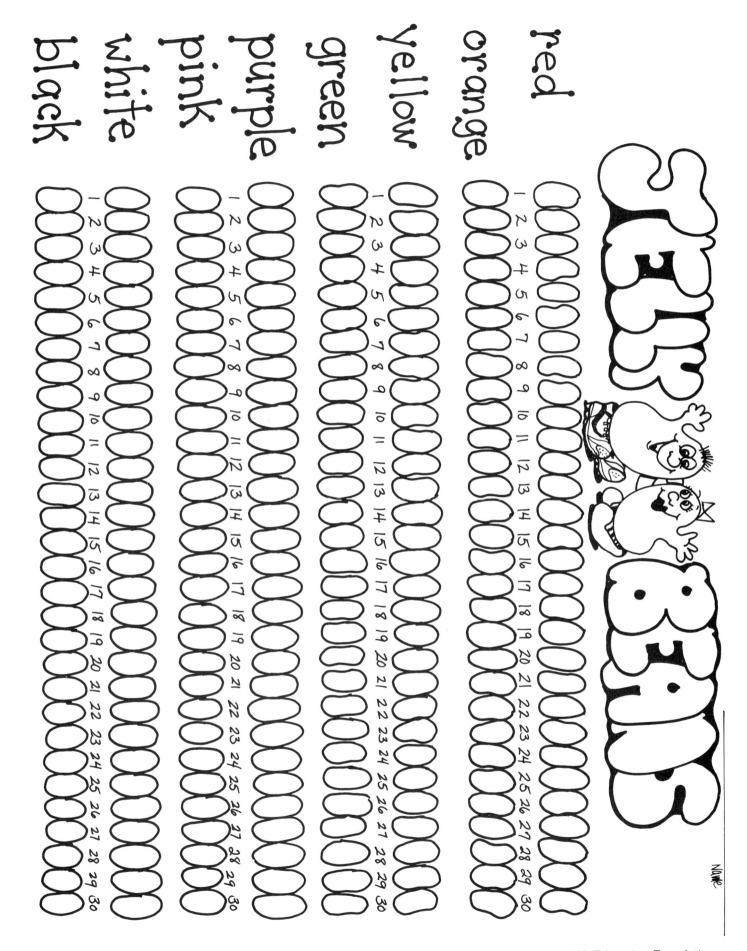

red

orange

yellow

green

purple

pink

white

black

The Jar That Likes to Keep You Guessing

I. Topic Area
Estimation and number concept.

II. Introductory Statement
Student will use a jar of small objects to build their skills in estimation, counting strategies and place value.

III. Math Skills / Science Processes

Math Skills	Science Processes
a. Estimating	a. Predicting
b. Counting	b. Collecting data
c. Place value	c. Comparing
d. Grouping	d. Generalizing
e. Problem solving	e. Applying information
f. Graphing	

IV. Materials
4–6 small Mason jars filled with jelly beans, walnuts, marbles, Teddy Bear counters, spools of thread, and pencil erasers (or similar objects).

V. Key Question
How many_____are in the jar?

VI. Background Information
1. Estimating is a skill each of us needs in order to function successfully. As adults we often use it without conscious effort. Our ability to estimate well improves with experience. Even as adults, we are uncomfortable and inaccurate when estimating very large or very small numbers. For example, can you picture a billion of something or describe a millionth of something?
2. To encourage youngsters to "guess", ask if they can estimate within 5 or 10 of the correct number rather than asking for the exact number.
3. This activity may be adapted to any grade level simply by selecting a range of numbers appropriate to that grade level. The process of grouping by two's, three's, etc. may be related to a number of concepts—addition, multiplication, place value, fair shares, and other number bases.

VII. Management Suggestions
1. For convenience and safety, keep the Guessing Jar at school. Have the youngsters bring from home objects to count in Ziplock baggies and then transfer them to the Guessing Jar.
2. Baby food jars may be substituted for small Mason jars.

VIII. Procedure
1. Begin by collecting a variety of small objects to be placed in the Guessing Jar. Duplicate the "home letter" and send the request home with each student. When the child returns with his contribution, transfer the objects to the "Guessing Jar."
2. Show the students the filled "Guessing Jar." Have the students estimate the number of objects in the jar while you record their estimates on the overhead, chalkboard, or large chart paper.
3. After 10-15 estimates have been recorded for all to see, ask very specific and creative questions about their estimates. For example: Does anyone see a number greater than 29? Is there a number with a 3 in the tens place? a 5 in the ones place? an odd number? and so forth. The kinds of questions asked will be determined by the appropriateness for the grade level.
4. Students may use the "Guessing Jar" recording pages to make a record of the counting methods used to count the objects in the jar.
5. On the first activity page, the student identifies the objects by naming them and then estimates the total number.
6. Draw a picture or sketch of the Guessing Jar.
7. The teacher pours out the contents of the Jar on the overhead or table nearby and leads the students in grouping the items by tens. You may wish to place each goup of ten objects into a paper cup. Then cout and record the number of tens and the number of ones. Discuss what happens if you reverse the number of tens and the number of ones.
8. Keep a daily record that shows a picture of the objects and the total number so that students can refer to past experience in making future estimates.
9. The second and third activity pages may be used to record estimates and place value counting methods for several different small jars of objects. One page is formatted with selected objects. The other is open-ended to include your choice of objects. Students work in small groups and record their estimates and then group by tens and ones as modeled by the teacher. Record in the appropriate place and exchange jars with another group. Continue until all jars have completed the rounds.
10. The fourth activity page allows youngsters to use the Guessing Jars to make fair shares. Students begin by identifying and naming the objects in the jar and recording their estimates of the total number.
11. Fair share the objects in the jar with two people (you and a friend). Record how many two's and how many left over. Then shade or color in the number of objects by two's in the grid. How many all together? Translate this information into mathematical language by filling in the equation: (_____ x 2) + _____ = _____.
12. Repeat a similar procedure for fair shares with three people, and with 5 people.

IX. Discussion Questions
Discussion questions of a specific nature have been included in the above described procedures. More general types of questions may be included in further discussion.
1. If the Guessing Jar is filled with objects that are smaller than the objects used today, will my estimate be higher or lower?
2. How does shape affect the number of objects in a jar?
3. Will a jar hold more marbles or more crayons?
4. What kinds of objects fill more space than others?
5. Can I fill *all* the space in a jar with "countable" objects?

X. Extension
1. When students become very confident, you may wish to combine more than one kind of item in the jar. For example, large marbles and small marbles.
2. At holidays, you may wish to fill a Jar with individually wrapped holiday candy for estimating and distributing for a treat.

Dear Parents,

This is a picture of the "jar that keeps us guessing." Please help your child find a number of small items that will fit in the jar (10-25 in the fall, 10-50 in the winter, 10-100 in the spring). Then, count the items with your child and send them to school in a plastic Zip Lock baggy.

Instruct your child not to tell anyone how many items are in the baggy.... not even their "best friend"! The class will transfer your contribution to the "jar" and will estimate the number of items in the jar. We will group them and count them in a variety of ways. Thank you for your help.

Your child's teacher,

─ Sample objects might include: ─

marbles	erasers	wooden blocks	pasta	jelly beans
pennies	pebbles	tiny toys	lima beans	sugar cubes
rice	BB's	sea shells	coffee beans	jelly bellies
beans	M&M's	pom poms	pinto beans	nuts, bolts
macaroni	buttons	gum balls	walnuts	washers
balls	cereals	candies	plastic beads	filberts
jacks	popcorn	small tiles	hazel nuts	raisins
peanuts	dice	styrofoam beads	game pieces	gummy bears

Guessing Jar

Today, our jar is keeping us guessing about _____ .

My guess is _____ .

This is a picture of the guessing jar and the _____ inside.

Make a record:

Tens	Ones

There were _____ tens and _____ ones.

All together there are _____ .

My guess is _____ more than we counted

or _____ less than we counted.

The number we counted is odd or even.

(circle one)

© 1987 AIMS Education Foundation

Guessing Jars

Name _____

 Jelly Beans

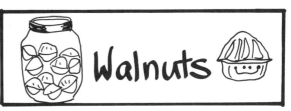 Walnuts

Guess: Total:

Tens	Ones

Guess: Total:

Tens	Ones

 Marbles

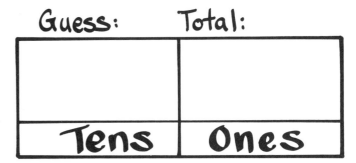 Teddy Bears

Guess: Total:

Tens	Ones

Guess: Total:

Tens	Ones

 Spools of Thread

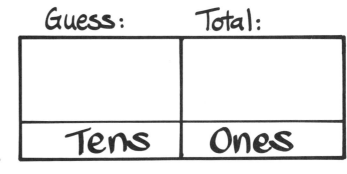 Pencil Erasers

Guess: Total:

Tens	Ones

Guess: Total:

Tens	Ones

More Guessing Jars

Guess: Total:

Tens	Ones

Guess: Total:

Tens	Ones

Guess: Total:

Tens	Ones

Guess: Total:

Tens	Ones

Guess: Total:

Tens	Ones

Guess: Total:

Tens	Ones

Guessing Jar - Making Fair Shares

Today, our jar is keeping us guessing about _____.

My estimate is _____.

1. Fair share the objects in the jar with 2 people (you and a friend).
How many twos? _____ How many left over? _____

Color in the number of twos and any left over.

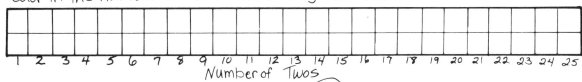

Number of Twos

• How many all together? _____ . (AHA!) (___ x 2) + ___ = _____

2. Fair share the objects in the jar with 3 people (you and 2 friends).
How many threes? _____ How many left over? _____

Color in the number of threes and any left over.

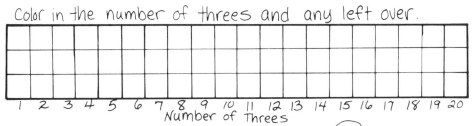

Number of Threes

• How many all together? _____ . (AHA) (___ x 3) + ___ = _____

3. Fair share the objects in the jar with 5 people (you and 4 friends).
How many fives? _____ How many left over? _____

Color in the number of fives and any left over

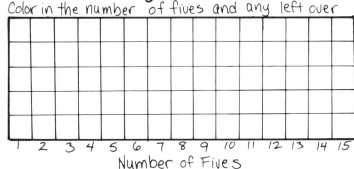

Number of Fives

• How many all together?
_____

(AHA) (___ x 5) + ___ = ___

Let Me Count the Ways

Topic
Measurement, direct comparison and non-customary units

Key Question
How should these objects be arranged to show lightest to heaviest?

Focus
The students will use the direct comparison of objects to order them from lightest to heaviest. They will also use non-customary units (Teddy Bear Counters) to compare the masses of the objects.

Guiding Documents
Project 2061 Benchmarks
- *Tools are used to do things better or more easily and to do some things that could not otherwise be done at all. In technology, tools are used to observe, measure, and make things.*
- *Simple graphs can help to tell about observations.*
- *Use whole numbers and simple, everyday fractions in ordering, counting, identifying, measuring, and describing things and experiences.*
- *Describe and compare things in terms of number, shape, texture, size, weight, color, and motion.*

NCR Standards
- *Employ simple equipment and tools to gather data and extend the senses.*
- *Objects have many observable properties, including size, weight, shape, color, temperature, and the ability to react with other substances. Those properties can be measured using tools, such as rulers, balances, and thermometers.*

NCTM Standards
- *Verify and interpret results with respect to the original problem*
- *Develop the process of measuring and concepts related to units of measurements*
- *Construct, read, and interpret displays of data*

Math
Counting
Measurement
   mass
Graphing
Estimating
Sequencing
Logic

Integrated Processes
Predicting
Observing
Comparing and contrasting
Communicating
Collecting and recording data
Interpreting data

Materials
Teddy Bear Counters
Balance
Scissors
Glue
Bag containing:
   eraser
   scissors
   box of eight crayons
   small block of wood
   tennis ball or small rubber
   small lump of clay

Background Information
Measurement in its simplest form is a direct comparison of one object to another to answer questions like: Which is more?... less?... the same? When direct comparisons are not accurate enough, a unit of measure becomes necessary. Because a unit such as a centimeter or a gram has very little meaning for a young child, uniform counted objects such as Teddy Bear Counters are used to build the idea of measurement.

Management
1. Six objects have been suggested for this activity. You may want to substitute or replace them with other objects. In this case, illustrations of the substituted objects would need to replace the pictures on the activity sheets. For very young learners, you may want to limit the number of objects used to three or four.
2. The activity is divided into two parts: Part *1* emphasizes the direct comparison of the objects by how they feel in the students' hands and how they compare to each other in the balance. *Part 2* uses a balance and Teddy Bear Counters to compare the masses of the objects.
3. Be aware that the strips for graphing that are supplied have only 12 spaces. If any object has a mass greater than 12 Teddy Bear Counters, two or more strips can be put together.
4. Students are asked to predict the order of the objects from light to heavy. If they experience difficulty in this sequencing process, you may want to teach them an organizational strategy such as:
   - Place six sheets of plain paper on the table. Indicate that the farthest sheet to the left (first paper) is for the lightest object and the farthest sheet to the right (sixth paper) is for the heaviest object. Allow time for the students to determine the lightest and heaviest object and to place them on the respective papers.
   - Ask them how many objects are remaining. [4] Have them determine which of the remaining objects are lightest and heaviest and place them on the appropriate papers (the second paper for the lightest of the four objects and the fifth paper for the heaviest).

- Ask them how many objects are now remaining. [2] Have them determine which of the remaining objects is lighter and which is heavier and place on the appropriate papers (the lighter of the two on the third paper and the heavier of the two on the fourth paper).
- All six objects will then be sequenced from lightest to heaviest.

5. Each group will need two colors of Teddy Bear Counters.

Procedure

Part 1

1. Distribute the first activity sheet. Have students cut out the first set of objects pictured under *My Hands*. Invite them to pick up the objects to determine the sequence of objects from lightest to heaviest. (See Management 3) Have them arrange and glue the pictures in order of the predicted sequence under *My Hands*.

2. Distribute a balance to each group. Ask them how they could use the balance, a tool of science, to determine the sequence of objects from lightest to heaviest. (One strategy is to try to find the heaviest object first, then the next heaviest, etc.) Allow time for them to test their ideas. Once they have used the balance, ask them to cut out and arrange the pictures of the objects from the pictures under *The Balance* in order from lightest to heaviest and glue them onto the first activity sheet under *The Balance*.

3. Allow students time to compare and contrast their results of My Hands and *The Balance*.

Part 2

1. Distribute the second activity sheet and have the students cut out the pictures of the six objects. Have them glue the pictures from lightest to heaviest using the information on the first activity page when they used the balance.

2. Inform students that now they are to select the lightest object and estimate how many Teddy Bear Counters it takes to equal its mass. Distribute a balance and the two colors of Teddy Bear Counters. Urge them to write in their prediction next to the picture of the lightest item.

3. Have students use the two colors of Teddy Bear counters to find the mass of the object. Direct them to count and record the two separate colors then add the two colors to get the total mass. It may be helpful if students use two crayons that match the colors of the Teddy Bear Counters to record the separate counts. For example: 4 red bears and 2 green bears— the numeral 4 is written with a red crayon while the numeral 2 is written in green. The total bears, 6, can be written with a pencil.

4. Once the actual results have been recorded, ask the students to estimate the mass of the next object. Once they have recorded their estimate, ask them to find its actual mass using the Teddy Bear Counters.

5. Repeat for all six objects.

6. Inform them that they will be making a bar graph that represents the number of Teddy Bear Counters they needed to use to equal the mass of each of the objects. Distribute the third activity sheet. Instruct students to use the two colors of their Teddy Bear Counters to color in the appropriate numbers of bears for each object. (For example: For the object used in the previous example that had a mass of 6 Teddy Bear Counters, they would color four bears red and two bears green.) Once the strips are colored, have them cut out the strips to the appropriate bear and arrange the strips from lightest objects to heaviest objects (fewest bears to most bears).

7. Direct them to glue the strips side-by-side to make a graph that shows the staircase effect produced when the objects are sequenced properly from lightest to heaviest.

Discussion

1. Which of the six objects was the lightest? Which was the heaviest? How do the strips show us which is heavier? ...lighter? ...same?

2. Which was easier to do, arrange the objects by lifting them with your hands or to use the balance? Explain.

3. Compare one object to another by asking, "Which object is heavier than the_____?" "What two objects had nearly the same mass?" "Which object has a mass of two (or other appropriate number) more bears than the_____?" "Which object has a mass of three (or other appropriate number) less bears than the?_____?"

4. Relate the graph, the series of strips, to ordering the objects from light to heavy. If the graph shows a staircase, each step getting higher, the sequence was accurate. The steps may not always be equal jumps, but they will always be upward, unless some of the objects have approximately the same mass.

Extensions

1. Have students color in another set of strips to make a class graph. Have students place their strips next to the appropriate *Graphing Label. Compare and contrast the results of each group for each object. The different combinations of addends represented by the two colors can be used to talk about the family of facts.* For example: 4 red bears and 2 green bears has the same sum as 2 blue bears and 4 yellow bears, and the same sum as 5 yellow bears and 1 red bear, etc.

2. Use the same procedure in *Part 2*, but use three colors of Teddy Bear Counters instead of the two.

3. Let students gather six different objects and sequence them from lightest to heaviest using the method of their choice.

crayons   *block*   *clay ball*

Let Me Count the Ways

Cut out the "My Hands" pictures. After you have picked up the objects glue the pictures in the chart from lightest to heaviest.

Cut out "The Balance" pictures. Use the balance to order the objects from lightest to heaviest.

Glue the pictures to show your results.

My Hand Lightest	The Balance Lightest

My Hand   The Balance

My Hand	The Balance
eraser	eraser
crayons	crayons
scissors	scissors
clay ball	clay ball
ball	ball
block	block

85

Let Me Count the Ways

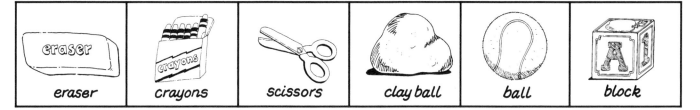

| eraser | crayons | scissors | clay ball | ball | block |

	My Guess	Find Mass and Count
	_____ bears	_____ + _____ = _____ bears
	_____ bears	_____ + _____ = _____ bears
	_____ bears	_____ + _____ = _____ bears
	_____ bears	_____ + _____ = _____ bears
	_____ bears	_____ + _____ = _____ bears
	_____ bears	_____ + _____ = _____ bears

Let Me Count the Ways ~ Graphing Strips

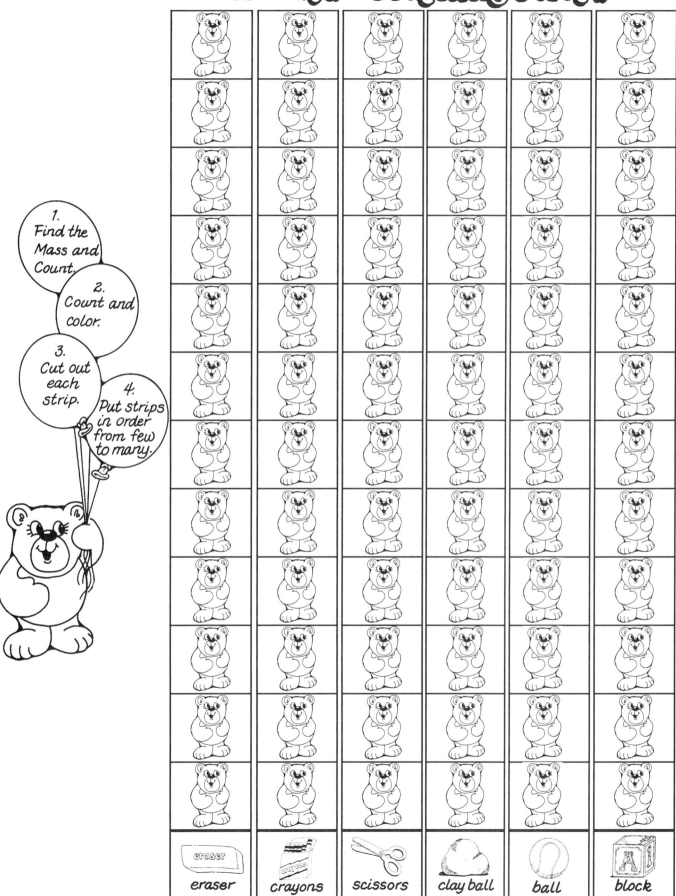

1. Find the Mass and Count.

2. Count and color.

3. Cut out each strip.

4. Put strips in order from few to many.

| eraser | crayons | scissors | clay ball | ball | block |

Let Me Count the Ways

1. Find the Mass and Count.

2. Count and Color.

3. Cut out each strip.

4. Put strips in order from few to many.

5. Glue the strips on another piece of paper.

| eraser | crayons | scissors | clay | tennis | block |

Let Me Count the Ways...

Children do not necessarily use "adult logic" in problem solving. Their thought processes are often very different from ours. Piaget and others suggest that children learn best by active participation on a concrete level, in a measurement activity where they have many opportunities for discussion and process reinforcement through repeated experiences with a variety of manipulatives.

Therefore, you may wish to use the open activity page and count the ways with....

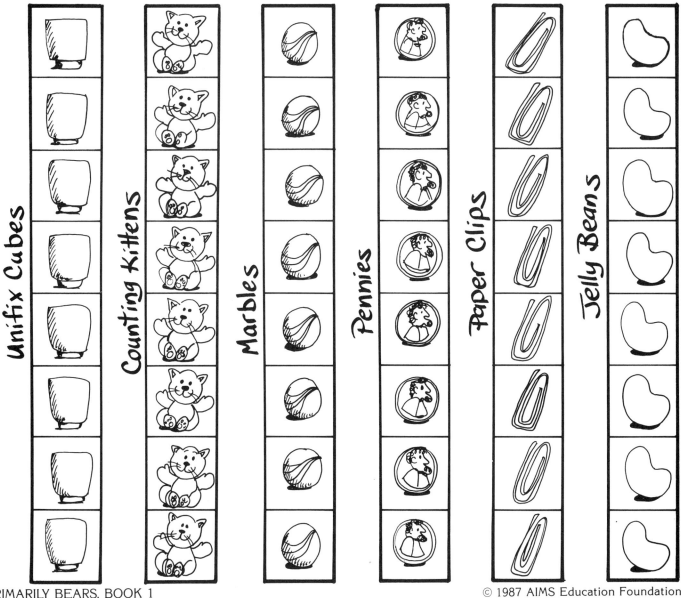

Unifix Cubes   Counting Kittens   Marbles   Pennies   Paper Clips   Jelly Beans

Let Me Count the Ways

eraser

crayons

scissors

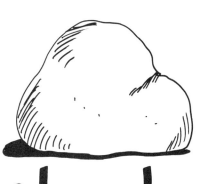
clay ball

tennis ball

wooden block

The AIMS Program

AIMS is the acronym for "Activities Integrating Mathematics and Science." Such integration enriches learning and makes it meaningful and holistic. AIMS began as a project of Fresno Pacific University to integrate the study of mathematics and science in grades K-9, but has since expanded to include language arts, social studies, and other disciplines.

AIMS is a continuing program of the non-profit AIMS Education Foundation. It had its inception in a National Science Foundation funded program whose purpose was to explore the effectiveness of integrating mathematics and science. The project directors in cooperation with 80 elemen-   tary classroom teachers devoted two years to a thorough field-testing of the results and implications of integration.

The approach met with such positive results that the decision was made to launch a program to create instructional materials incorporating this concept. Despite the fact that thoughtful educators have long recommended an integrative approach, very little appropriate material was available in 1981 when the project began. A series of writing projects have ensued and today the AIMS Education Foundation is committed to continue the creation of new integrated activities on a permanent basis.

The AIMS program is funded through the sale of this developing series of books and proceeds from the Foundation's endowment. All net income from program and products flows into a trust fund administered by the AIMS Education Foundation. Use of these funds is restricted to support of research, development, and publication of new materials. Writers donate all their rights to the Foundation to support its on-going program. No royalties are paid to the writers.

The rationale for integration lies in the fact that science, mathematics, language arts, social studies, etc., are integrally interwoven in the real world from which it follows that they should be similarly treated in the classroom where we are preparing students to live in that world. Teachers who use the AIMS program give enthusiastic endorsement to the effectiveness of this approach.

Science encompasses the art of questioning, investigating, hypothesizing, discovering, and communicating. Mathematics is a language that provides clarity, objectivity, and understanding. The language arts provide us powerful tools of communication. Many of the major contemporary societal issues stem from advancements in science and must be studied in the context of the social sciences. Therefore, it is timely that all of us take seriously a more holistic mode of educating our students. This goal motivates all who are associated with the AIMS Program. We invite you to join us in this effort.

Meaningful integration of knowledge is a major recommendation coming from the nation's professional science and mathematics associations. The American Association for the Advancement of Science in *Science for All Americans* strongly recommends the integration of mathematics, science, and technology. The National Council of Teachers of Mathematics places strong emphasis on applications of mathematics such as are found in science investigations. AIMS is fully aligned with these recommendations.

Extensive field testing of AIMS investigations confirms these beneficial results.

1. Mathematics becomes more meaningful, hence more useful, when it is applied to situations that interest students.
2. The extent to which science is studied and understood is increased, with a significant economy of time, when mathematics and science are integrated.
3. There is improved quality of learning and retention, supporting the thesis that learning which is meaningful and relevant is more effective.
4. Motivation and involvement are increased dramatically as students investigate real-world situations and participate actively in the process.

We invite you to become part of this classroom teacher movement by using an integrated approach to learning and sharing any suggestions you may have. The AIMS Program welcomes you!

AIMS Education Foundation Programs

A Day with AIMS

Intensive one-day workshops are offered to introduce educators to the philosophy and rationale of AIMS. Participants will discuss the methodology of AIMS and the strategies by which AIMS principles may be incorporated into curriculum. Each participant will take part in a variety of hands-on AIMS investigations to gain an understanding of such aspects as the scientific/mathematical content, classroom management, and connections with other curricular areas. *A Day with AIMS* workshops may be offered anywhere in the United States. Necessary supplies and take-home materials are usually included in the enrollment fee.

A Week with AIMS

Throughout the nation, AIMS offers many one-week workshops each year, usually in the summer. Each workshop lasts five days and includes at least 30 hours of AIMS hands-on instruction. Participants are grouped according to the grade level(s) in which they are interested. Instructors are members of the AIMS Instructional Leadership Network. Supplies for the activities and a generous supply of take-home materials are included in the enrollment fee. Sites are selected on the basis of applications submitted by educational organizations. If chosen to host a workshop, the host agency agrees to provide specified facilities and cooperate in the promotion of the workshop. The AIMS Education Foundation supplies workshop materials as well as the travel, housing, and meals for instructors.

AIMS One-Week Perspectives Workshops

Each summer, Fresno Pacific University offers AIMS one-week workshops on its campus in Fresno, California. AIMS Program Directors and highly qualified members of the AIMS National Leadership Network serve as instructors.

The Science Festival and the Festival of Mathematics

Each summer, Fresno Pacific University offers a Science Festival and a Festival of Mathematics. These festivals have gained national recognition as inspiring and challenging experiences, giving unique opportunities to experience hands-on mathematics and science in topical and grade-level groups. Guest faculty includes some of the nation's most highly regarded mathematics and science educators. Supplies and take-home materials are included in the enrollment fee.

The AIMS Instructional Leadership Program

This is an AIMS staff-development program seeking to prepare facilitators for leadership roles in science/math education in their home districts or regions. Upon successful completion of the program, trained facilitators may become members of the AIMS Instructional Leadership Network, qualified to conduct AIMS workshops, teach AIMS in-service courses for college credit, and serve as AIMS consultants. Intensive training is provided in mathematics, science, process and thinking skills, workshop management, and other relevant topics.

College Credit and Grants

Those who participate in workshops may often qualify for college credit. If the workshop takes place on the campus of Fresno Pacific University, that institution may grant appropriate credit. If the workshop takes place off-campus, arrangements can sometimes be made for credit to be granted by another institution. In addition, the applicant's home school district is often willing to grant in-service or professional-development credit. Many educators who participate in AIMS workshops are recipients of various types of educational grants, either local or national. Nationally known foundations and funding agencies have long recognized the value of AIMS mathematics and science workshops to educators. The AIMS Education Foundation encourages educators interested in attending or hosting workshops to explore the possibilities suggested above. Although the Foundation strongly supports such interest, it reminds applicants that they have the primary responsibility for fulfilling *current* requirements.

For current information regarding the programs described above, please complete the following:

Information Request

Please send current information on the items checked:

___ *Basic Information Packet* on AIMS materials	___ *AIMS One-Week Perspectives* workshops
___ *Festival of Mathematics*	___ *A Week with AIMS* workshops
___ *Science Festival*	___ Hosting information for *A Day with AIMS* workshops
___ *AIMS Instructional Leadership Program*	___ Hosting information for *A Week with AIMS* workshops

Name _____ Phone _____

Address _____

      Street   City   State   Zip

AIMS Program Publications

GRADES K-4 SERIES

Bats Incredible!
Brinca de Alegria Hacia la Primavera con las Matemáticas y Ciencias
Cáete de Gusto Hacia el Otoño con la Matemática y Ciencias
Cycles of Knowing and Growing
Fall Into Math and Science
Field Detectives
Glide Into Winter With Math and Science
Hardhatting in a Geo-World (Revised Edition, 1996)
Jaw Breakers and Heart Thumpers (Revised Edition, 1995)
Los Cincos Sentidos
Overhead and Underfoot (Revised Edition, 1994)
Patine al Invierno con Matemáticas y Ciencias
Popping With Power (Revised Edition, 1996)
Primariamente Física (Revised Edition, 1994)
Primarily Earth
Primariamente Plantas
Primarily Physics (Revised Edition, 1994)
Primarily Plants
Sense-able Science
Spring Into Math and Science
Under Construction

GRADES K-6 SERIES

Budding Botanist
Critters
El Botanista Principiante
Exploring Environments
Mostly Magnets
Ositos Nada Más
Primarily Bears
Principalmente Imanes
Water Precious Water

GRADES 5-9 SERIES

Actions with Fractions
Brick Layers
Brick Layers II
Conexiones Eléctricas
Down to Earth
Electrical Connections
Finding Your Bearings (Revised Edition, 1996)
Floaters and Sinkers (Revised Edition, 1995)
From Head to Toe
Fun With Foods
Gravity Rules!
Historical Connections in Mathematics, Volume I
Historical Connections in Mathematics, Volume II
Historical Connections in Mathematics, Volume III
Just for the Fun of It!
Machine Shop
Magnificent Microworld Adventures
Math + Science, A Solution
Off the Wall Science: A Poster Series Revisited
Our Wonderful World
Out of This World (Revised Edition, 1994)
Pieces and Patterns, A Patchwork in Math and Science
Piezas y Diseños, un Mosaic de Matemáticas y Ciencias
Proportional Reasoning
Soap Films and Bubbles
Spatial Visualization
The Sky's the Limit (Revised Edition, 1994)
The Amazing Circle, Volume 1
Through the Eyes of the Explorers:
    Minds-on Math & Mapping
What's Next, Volume 1
What's Next, Volume 2
What's Next, Volume 3

For further information write to:

AIMS Education Foundation • P.O. Box 8120 • Fresno, California 93747-8120
www.AIMSedu.org/ • Fax 559•255•6396

We invite you to subscribe to 𝒜𝐼𝑀𝑆!

Each issue of 𝒜𝐼𝑀𝑆 contains a variety of material useful to educators at all grade levels. Feature articles of lasting value deal with topics such as mathematical or science concepts, curriculum, assessment, the teaching of process skills, and historical background. Several of the latest AIMS math/science investigations are always included, along with their reproducible activity sheets. As needs direct and space allows, various issues contain news of current developments, such as workshop schedules, activities of the AIMS Instructional Leadership Network, and announcements of upcoming publications.

𝒜𝐼𝑀𝑆 is published monthly, August through May. Subscriptions are on an annual basis only. A subscription entered at any time will begin with the next issue, but will also include the previous issues of that volume. Readers have preferred this arrangement because articles and activities within an annual volume are often interrelated.

Please note that an 𝒜𝐼𝑀𝑆 subscription automatically includes duplication rights for one school site for all issues included in the subscription. Many schools build cost-effective library resources with their subscriptions.

YES! I am interested in subscribing to 𝒜𝐼𝑀𝑆.

Name _____   Home Phone _____

Address _____   City, State, Zip _____

Please send the following volumes (subject to availability):

_____	Volume V	(1990-91)	$30.00	_____ Volume X	(1995-96)	$30.00
_____	Volume VI	(1991-92)	$30.00	_____ Volume XI	(1996-97)	$30.00
_____	Volume VII	(1992-93)	$30.00	_____ Volume XII	(1997-98)	$30.00
_____	Volume VIII	(1993-94)	$30.00	_____ Volume XIII	(1998-99)	$30.00
_____	Volume IX	(1994-95)	$30.00	_____ Volume XIV	(1999-00)	$30.00

_____ **Limited offer: Volumes XIV & XV (1999-2001) $55.00**
(Note: Prices may change without notice)

Check your method of payment:

❏ Check enclosed in the amount of $ _____

❏ Purchase order attached (Please include the P.O.#, the authorizing signature, and position of the authorizing person.)

❏ Credit Card   ❏ Visa   ❏ MasterCard   Amount $ _____

Card # _____   Expiration Date _____

Signature _____   Today's Date _____

Make checks payable to **AIMS Education Foundation.**
Mail to 𝒜𝐼𝑀𝑆 Magazine, P.O. Box 8120, Fresno, CA 93747-8120.
Phone (559) 255-4094 or (888) 733-2467 FAX (559) 255-6396
AIMS Homepage: http://www.AIMSedu.org/

AIMS Duplication Rights Program

AIMS has received many requests from school districts for the purchase of unlimited duplication rights to AIMS materials. In response, the AIMS Education Foundation has formulated the program outlined below. There is a built-in flexibility which, we trust, will provide for those who use AIMS materials extensively to purchase such rights for either individual activities or entire books.

It is the goal of the AIMS Education Foundation to make its materials and programs available at reasonable cost. All income from the sale of publications and duplication rights is used to support AIMS programs; hence, strict adherence to regulations governing duplication is essential. Duplication of AIMS materials beyond limits set by copyright laws and those specified below is strictly forbidden.

Limited Duplication Rights

Any purchaser of an AIMS book may make up to *200 copies* of any activity in that book for use at *one school site*. Beyond that, rights must be purchased according to the appropriate category.

Unlimited Duplication Rights for Single Activities

An individual or school may purchase the right to make an unlimited number of copies of a single activity. The royalty is $5.00 per activity per school site.

Examples: 3 activities x 1 site x $5.00 = $15.00
9 activities x 3 sites x $5.00 = $135.00

Unlimited Duplication Rights for Entire Books

A school or district may purchase the right to make an unlimited number of copies of a single, *specified* book. The royalty is $20.00 per book per school site. This is in addition to the cost of the book.

Examples: 5 books x 1 site x $20.00 = $100.00
12 books x 10 sites x $20.00 = $2400.00

Magazine/Newsletter Duplication Rights

Those who purchase *AIMS* (magazine)/*Newsletter* are hereby granted permission to make up to 200 copies of any portion of it, provided these copies will be used for educational purposes.

Workshop Instructors' Duplication Rights

Workshop instructors may distribute to registered workshop participants a maximum of 100 copies of any article and/or 100 copies of no more than eight activities, provided these six conditions are met:

1. Since all AIMS activities are based upon the *AIMS Model of Mathematics* and the *AIMS Model of Learning*, leaders must include in their presentations an explanation of these two models.
2. Workshop instructors must relate the AIMS activities presented to these basic explanations of the AIMS philosophy of education.
3. The copyright notice must appear on all materials distributed.
4. Instructors must provide information enabling participants to order books and magazines from the Foundation.
5. Instructors must inform participants of their limited duplication rights as outlined below.
6. Only student pages may be duplicated.

Written permission must be obtained for duplication beyond the limits listed above. Additional royalty payments may be required.

Workshop Participants' Rights

Those enrolled in workshops in which AIMS student activity sheets are distributed may duplicate a maximum of 35 copies or enough to use the lessons one time with one class, whichever is less. Beyond that, rights must be purchased according to the appropriate category.

Application for Duplication Rights

The purchasing agency or individual must clearly specify the following:
1. Name, address, and telephone number
2. Titles of the books for Unlimited Duplication Rights contracts
3. Titles of activities for Unlimited Duplication Rights contracts
4. Names and addresses of school sites for which duplication rights are being purchased.

NOTE: Books to be duplicated must be purchased separately and are not included in the contract for Unlimited Duplication Rights.

The requested duplication rights are automatically authorized when proper payment is received, although a *Certificate of Duplication Rights* will be issued when the application is processed.

Address all correspondence to: **Contract Division**
AIMS Education Foundation
P.O. Box 8120
Fresno, CA 93747-8120

www.AIMSedu.org/
Fax 559•255•6396